bespoke

FURNITURE FROM 101
INTERNATIONAL ARTISTS

E. ASHLEY ROONEY

WITH CONTRIBUTIONS BY
Gary Inman, Thomas Throop, & Lewis Wexler

Schiffer Publishing Ltd

4880 Lower Valley Road • Atglen, PA 19310

Copyright © 2012 by E. Ashley Rooney

Library of Congress Control Number: 2012946105

All rights reserved. No part of this work may be reproduced or used in any form or by any means—graphic, electronic, or mechanical, including photocopying or information storage and retrieval systems—without written permission from the publisher.

The scanning, uploading and distribution of this book or any part thereof via the Internet or via any other means without the permission of the publisher is illegal and punishable by law. Please purchase only authorized editions and do not participate in or encourage the electronic piracy of copyrighted materials.

"Schiffer," "Schiffer Publishing Ltd. & Design," and the "Design of pen and inkwell" are registered trademarks of Schiffer Publishing Ltd.

Designed by Justin Watkinson
Type set in Futura Std/Zurich BT

ISBN: 978-0-7643-4226-4
Printed in China

Credits. Front cover (L to R): Brian Fireman (Michael Traister), John & Andrea Hartcorn (Eric Limon), Alun Heslop (Sylvain Deleu), George Mahoney Fredrick Vogt (Dennis McWaters) Lex Stobie Andrew Lloyd), Peter Harrison, (StockStudiosPhotography.com), Brian Fireman (Michael Traister), Tom Huang with Andrew Williams, David Emery (Mark Ashkanasy), Carlos Motta (Fernando Laszlo), and William Acland. **Back cover:** Henry Pilcher (Michelle Taylor), Paring Dovetails (David Redpath), David Hurd with Gravitas. **Copyright page:** Roger Heitzman. **Title page:** Alun Heslop (Sylvain Deleu). **Flaps:** David Emery with Peter Cole (John Brash). Chapter starts: Jules Siegel (D. Peter Lund), p.9; David Ebner (Stephen Amiaga), p.49; Brian Fireman (Michael Traister), p.83; Tim Gorman (Ramon Moreno Photography), p.101; David Rasmussen (David Rasmussen Design), p.125; Jeff O'Brien, p.141; William Acland, p.165.

Schiffer Books are available at special discounts for bulk purchases for sales promotions or premiums. Special editions, including personalized covers, corporate imprints, and excerpts can be created in large quantities for special needs. For more information contact the publisher:

Published by Schiffer Publishing Ltd.
4880 Lower Valley Road
Atglen, PA 19310
Phone: (610) 593-1777; Fax: (610) 593-2002
E-mail: Info@schifferbooks.com

For the largest selection of fine reference books on this and related subjects, please visit our website at **www.schifferbooks.com**
We are always looking for people to write books on new and related subjects. If you have an idea for a book, please contact us at proposals@schifferbooks.com

This book may be purchased from the publisher.
Please try your bookstore first.
You may write for a free catalog.

In Europe, Schiffer books are distributed by
Bushwood Books
6 Marksbury Ave.
Kew Gardens
Surrey TW9 4JF England
Phone: 44 (0) 20 8392 8585; Fax: 44 (0) 20 8392 9876
E-mail: info@bushwoodbooks.co.uk
Website: www.bushwoodbooks.co.uk

Acknowledgments

The creative act never ceases to amaze me; each new book is an experience, an adventure, and a challenge. There is a reason why I selected these artisans for this book. They do classy work.

It was the work of an artisan, Jules Siegel that triggered this work. He introduced me to the beauty of bespoke or studio furniture. Some call it one-of-a-kind, which it truly is.

Gary Inman, Thomas Throop, and Lewis Wexler added some phenomenal talent to this book. I have worked with Gary before and am delighted to include his insights here. I had not worked with Thomas Throop or Lewis Wexler before, but I knew their reputation and I have learned a great deal from them.

Schiffer's graphics artists make the book beautiful. Finally, I am a fortunate woman to know Barbara Purchia, who does that final review of the manuscript.

Contents

Preface

E. Ashley Rooney

I grew up in Connecticut surrounded by furniture from Mississippi, Kentucky, and Pennsylvania. My parents loved their heritage, and their furniture showed it. The long walnut refractory table, which had stood in a Philadelphia front hall, became my father's desk; my Kentucky grandmother's Empire mahogany chest of drawers, c. 1830, now belonged to my mother, while the uncomfortable mahogany sofa with the scrolled crest rail sat in front of the television – one way of making TV-watching more uncomfortable. My mother revered this furniture; it was part of the family's mystique.

These hand built pieces are endowed with an inimitable allure. Their presence evokes the past and the stories of those former family members. Others were transformed to provide style in a more contemporary environment. The only room in our house that didn't have one of the pieces was the dining room. By her late 60s, my mother saved up enough money to have a cherry dining room table designed by a Connecticut craftsperson. She bought the chairs and had all the women in the family make needlepoint seats. Luckily, I was off in college.

Much later in life, my friend Jules Siegel reintroduced me to the work of furniture artisans. Today, custom-built furniture is no longer just wood, but steel, bamboo, fiberglass, nori, epoxy resin, etc. The twenty-first century craftsman uses modern tools to bring out the natural beauty of these substances, creating furniture with artistic flair to meet the needs of this generation.

This book is unique for me in that I drew on the talents and knowledge of three experts: Gary Inman, a designer; Thomas Throop, an artisan; and Lewis Wexler, an art expert.

Some of these 98 artisans have been in the field for several decades; others are newly emerging. All are skilled in the techniques of their trade yet have the creativity to design handcrafted furniture that offers great beauty.

These artisans from throughout the United States and the world:

- Produce distinctive furniture that reflects the work of the fine craftsman of the past, the ideas of the future, and, in some cases, their region

- Seek to perfect materials, forms, and finishes to meet the individual needs of their clients

- Love working with their hands.

"My furniture refused to stay furniture. It spoke in ironic quips. It asked questions. It made statements," David Michael Redwine, who is seen pairing dovetails.

A graduate of Rhode Island School of Design, Adam Curtis has a full-time day job for the Town of Lexington and does commission work in the furniture design field in his spare time. This is his Dragon Table.

Foreword

The Life of a Piece

Thomas Throop

As a furniture designer and maker, I am fascinated by the limitless options that are presented to me every day. The choices are staggering. What wood to use, what is the appropriate grain pattern, the speed of a curve, the proportion, the shape, the symmetry, the joinery, the function… what am I trying to express, what are the needs to be served by the piece? It is the culmination of these choices that form a story about each piece of furniture and its maker.

A piece of furniture evolves. It might start as a formal brief from a client meeting or a rough sketch on the back of an envelope, then it could move to a mock up or scale model, progress to a variety of parts, and finally be assembled into a finished piece. Most importantly, it finds a home where it begins a new life and starts a new chapter in its story. It is a process, an incubation of ideas and a calculation of what is possible. There is a call and response in which the path of the piece can change at any turn. There is great freedom, though it is not without constraint. The piece has to work. It must be structurally sound and function as expected, but it also must convey the intended expression and character.

The ultimate value of a piece lies in the maker and the making, but also in the life the piece leads once it is out in the world. I often think of the house in which my grandmother lived and the unusual antique pieces with which she surrounded herself. She had a pretty good eye, and she took great pride in those pieces and enjoyed recounting how she happened to come to have them. Her taste was somewhat eclectic, but there seemed to be a theme and quiet inevitability in her choices that ran through the house. Most had been found at country auctions and a few at fine dealers. Some pieces had been handed down through the family, and these provided a valuable connection to my family's story and a glimpse of life in an earlier time. Regardless, each had its own unique story. These pieces came to have a mystique about them, and it was clear that the value in possessing them was as much about the story as it was the beauty of the piece itself. There is something special about how people define themselves with their surroundings and how their furniture might define them and our memories of them.

I think of this often when I am making a piece for a client. It helps remind me that the story of how the piece comes about is as important as the piece itself, both for me and for the family in which the piece ultimately ends up.

The excellence and diversity of furniture featured in this book exemplifies the unique and individual stories of the makers and the endless choices they make every day. The process can be a valuable expression in and of itself, and the end result can be a story to be passed on from one generation to the next.

Thomas Throop has been designing and making one-off furniture for nearly 20 years. Formally trained in England at the John Makepeace School for Craftsmen in Wood, he works primarily to commission. He has exhibited his furniture in over 90 juried exhibitions, including the Smithsonian Craft Show and the Philadelphia Museum and has won numerous awards such as the Wharton Esherick Prize. His furniture has been featured in many publications, Dona Meilach's Wood Art Today, Kerry Pierce's Custom Furniture Source Book – A Guide to 125 Craftsman, and House and Garden Magazine. Public collections include The White House Ornament Collection in Washington DC. Tom's work has been exhibited in various galleries across the US and in London, England. In 2011, Tom was invited to curate an exhibition of studio furniture, "The Next Wave: A third generation of studio furniture makers," at the Windsor Art Center. His studio, Black Creek Designs LLC, is located in the village center of New Canaan, CT.

The Bespoke Design Process

Gary Inman

Bespoke design is a pas de deux between designer and client; between form and function. It is the marriage of creativity and practicality, resulting in a beautiful, purposeful, and, above all, unique art object. When clients commission an artist to create an heirloom that grows out of their personal vision and their pragmatic needs, they begin a journey that will ideally end with the realization of that vision. The process of creating a bespoke object can appear daunting, but if one follows the three essential steps the process need not be stressful.

The first, and the most critical step, is to clearly define your vision and your needs to the designer. Think of descriptive words that capture the essence of the piece you have in mind. Is it rustic or elegant, grand and dramatic, or understated and subtle? This step in the process is often referred to as programming. It is essentially the creation of a list of desires and functions. How large does the piece need to be? What purpose will it serve? What types of materials are preferred? Is it to be crafted of wood or forged in metal? Will it feature glass or stone or another material for contrast to the main material? Will it be dark and ponderous or light and ephemeral? With bespoke design, there need be no limitations. Typically, designers prepare a list of questions based upon design parameters that they will try to obtain from the programming interview. The bespoke process normally requires continual dialogue between client and designer throughout the journey, but the first fact-finding session is the most critical to the success of the project.

Once the designer has an initial program, he/she will begin creating schematic sketches. These hand sketches are meant to capture the spirit of the piece as described by the client. There are routinely several loose sketches at this stage to determine a direction. The preliminary sketches may actually begin during the programming session as the client describes their dream creation. An astute artist may be able to leave the first meeting with the core design in hand. It is necessary to have a follow-up session to review and edit the schematic or conceptual designs and agree upon a singular direction that the designer will develop further. Indecisiveness at this stage can be detrimental to the successful completion of the commission. It is always critical to do your homework and have a clearly defined goal before kicking off the design process. This prevents frustration and cost inefficiencies for both members of the team.

Bespoke design can be very diverse in medium from hand-tufted or knotted rugs to lighting fixtures, textiles, wallpapers, passementerie, upholstery, and, of course, furniture.

Bespoke design affords a unique opportunity to share a story, ideally a story that captures the client's personal journey in a meaningful way. Family history, travel tales, and lifestyle aspirations can be woven into tangible form. Perfectly fitting the design context is another advantage of bespoke design. Color palettes, scale, and rare materials can add mystery to a home that is impossible to achieve with standard production furniture.

A recent commission for dining chairs in a large Tudor-Gothic style home presented a scale challenge. The solution was to have extra tall chairs to counterbalance the ceiling height of thirteen feet and the unusually high paneling. Guests feel comforted by the cozy candlelit cocoon rather than feeling lost in the over scaled Gothic room.

The Edward chair uses leather for the seat, a practical design solution for the dining room. It has pleated suede for the base panel and chair back. Its size helps to create a space within a space.

Introduction

The adjoining sitting room also benefitted from custom scaling with a pair of unique Obie chairs, which draw their inspiration from Japanese costumes with a sash of aqua being inspired by the large over-mantle painting. The bespoke Mutes coffee table gives new meaning to the phrase "conversation piece," as it was fabricated in India by the descendents of the artisans that built the iconic Taj Mahal. Crafting a special story for an object can communicate the owner's interests in a powerful way.

Design development is the second key step in the bespoke process. Armed with an approved schematic design sketch, the designer works to refine that concept into a buildable piece of furniture. At this stage of development, the use of computer-assisted design comes into play. The artist, or their draftsperson, will convert the hand sketch into working drawings that include plans, elevations, and sections. Detail studies may be required if the piece is more complex. This phase is critical, as it results in the creation of drawings that will guide fabricators in creating the actual piece. These working drawings allow the designer and their designated workshop to evaluate dimensional systems from both an aesthetic and structural perspective. Correct proportional relationships must be maintained if the piece is to be visually pleasing, but you can never lose sight of the structural requirements. Here, again, the programming notes come into play, as designer and fabricator balance the functional needs and aesthetic desires in the final design.

The material palette is also decided upon at this stage of the process. The designer will present options to their client and will begin to acquire cost estimates for those materials. Ideally the duet, designer and client, have agreed upon a budget at the onset of the commission to prevent value engineering later in the process. The design development stage concludes with a thorough review of all aspects of the design. Again, the client is asked to approve the proposed design in order to move it to the final stage of the process, production.

In the third and final step in the journey, the designer works closely with the selected fabricator to refine the design.

Descendents of the Taj Mahal artisans fabricated the Mumtaz Coffee Table; Virginian metalsmiths forged its base. Inman designed both. In the far left corner is the Obi chair, scaled to the high paneling and tall ceiling.

Furniture makers are able to draw upon their experience to recommend ways to improve and bring greater efficiency to the design. A professional fabricator will create shop drawings based upon the designer's plans. Shop drawings offer even greater detail in terms of the construction methods to be used and must be carefully reviewed and approved by the artist before production begins. Finishes and materials are finalized at this stage, as unique materials may require time to arrive in the workroom. Some workshops will provide a model as a part of the shop drawing submittal. Once shop drawings are approved, the piece goes into production and may require several weeks to as much as a year to complete, depending upon the material medium and skill level required.

A successful dance partnership between the client and designer will result in a piece of furniture that celebrates the owner's original vision and hopefully surpasses his/her highest aspirations. Bespoke furniture becomes an instant family heirloom that promises to bring enjoyment and a great family story to future generations.

Bibliography:

Brèon, Emmanuel and Rosalind Pepall, Editors. *Ruhlmann, Genius of Art Deco*. Paris: Somogy èditions d'art. 2004.

Linley, David. *Design and Detail in the Home*. New York: Harry N. Abrams, Inc. Publishers. 2000.

Gary Inman is an accomplished furniture and interior designer with an impressive portfolio of east coast projects. He is Principal and Director of the Hotel and Home Design Studio at Glavé & Holmes Architecture in Richmond, Virginia. A dynamic interpreter of classic design, Mr. Inman is skilled at combining elements from the past with the best of contemporary design. He merges his lifelong appreciation of beauty with his scholarly understanding of architecture and antiquities. He is an award-winning designer, author, and frequent lecturer, whose work has been published in The Washington Post, Southern Accents, Traditional Homes, Home & Design and many others. Inman has also appeared on the popular cable series "America's Castles" and the PBS series "Monuments and Mansions."

1 New England

New England

Timothy Coleman

Shelburne, Massachusetts

"Fall Front." English sycamore and walnut. 25" x 57" x 15". 2006. *Copyright © Bill Truslow.*

My passion for creating beautiful things in wood began nearly forty years ago. It is what I was always meant to do.

As a twelve-year-old, while other kids were playing Little League baseball, I was busy in my makeshift workshop in the basement. A decade later, I was an apprentice to a master furniture maker in Seattle, then studied at the College of the Redwoods with James Krenov. In 1989, I returned to New England where I have been designing and building furniture ever since.

I live out in the country where I can see deep into the night sky. There is a rushing brook that cuts a wide path around my property. I marvel at the cycles of the seasons, observing the complexity of a dahlia blossom, the stripped down winter landscape, the multitude of stars in the sky. My observations often spark an idea for a furniture form, a surface pattern, or a detail. I make rough sketches, often sitting with an idea for months before something emerges as a workable concept.

I am fascinated with patterns, and I am always experimenting with different surface treatments as a way to incorporate patterns in my work. Some are traditional methods such as marquetry and low-relief carving, but I have also developed innovative techniques using embossing, parquet wood tiles, and scroll-sawn fretwork. The patterns add depth, texture, and complexity to the pieces.

I am drawn to forms that are spare in their lines but not stark. I love working shapes and surfaces by eye and by hand, creating subtle variations that give my pieces a lively energy. My furniture is described as poetic, graceful, and exquisitely detailed. For me, it's a reflection of the beauty I see in the world every day.

"Heaven and Earth." English brown oak, English sycamore, and roasted ash. 20" x 50" x 15". 2010. *Courtesy of Dean Powell Photography.*

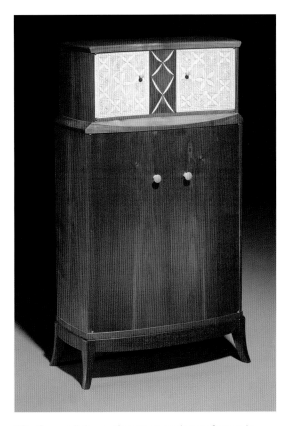

"So Sweet." Argentine rose cedar, soft maple, and jatoba. 26" x 43" x 12". 2005. *Courtesy of Dean Powell Photography.*

"Key to My Heart." Japanese ash and imbuya. 23" x 39" x 15". 2009. *Courtesy of Dean Powell Photography.*

"Yew and Me." Yew, English sycamore, and imbuya. 32" x 60" x 14". 2003.

With the wall cabinet, "Leap and the Net Will Appear." Courtesy of Clements/Howcroft.

Mark Del Guidice

Norwood, Massachusetts

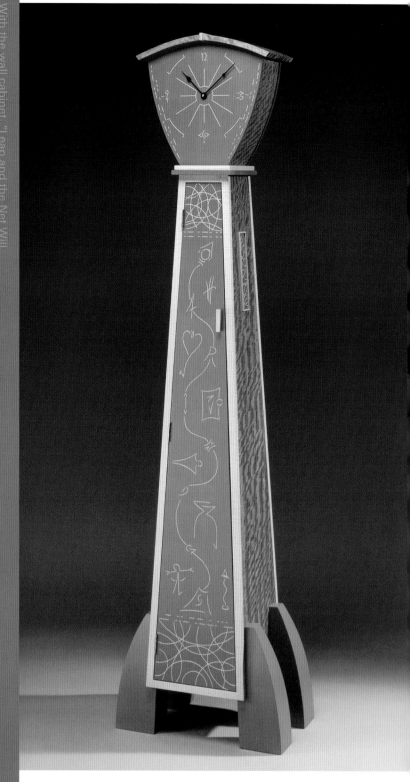

"Time's Up Case Clock." Bubinga veneer, curly maple, basswood, quartz clock movement, milk paint, and varnish. Carved with intuitive hieroglyphs and Morse code, which reads "Time's Up." 21" x 80" x 14". 2004. *Courtesy of Clements/Howcroft.*

My interest in furniture making was sparked when I created some simple utilitarian pieces for my college apartment. I constructed a bed, a desk, and, of course, the all-important stereo cabinet. After all, it was the seventies.

Over time, I came to realize that my management career would not be as rewarding as working with my hands, so I set off on an exploration of furniture making that has brought me to today's intersection of art, craft, and design.

When I began this venture, I had immediate good fortune when I discovered the Artisanry program at Boston University. My exposure there helped me develop a strong visual vocabulary and the woodworking skills necessary to execute my unique personal expression.

Through all the years since, I have followed a lot of paths opened up by various commissions and opportunities that came my way. They have often required learning new skills, while providing me with new perspectives. These experiences have also informed my parallel pursuit of artistic expression in speculative pieces of furniture.

Currently, some of my creative focus is in drawing and carving what I call intuitive hieroglyphs. These are the images incised in some of the surfaces of my work. I generate these hieroglyphs by drawing in my sketchbook from an unintentional perspective, allowing for the expression of internalized images in new and simplified ways.

Over time, I have developed a vocabulary of these symbols. Interestingly, I find that despite what these images mean to me, they evoke different personal interpretations from each person that views them, underscoring the interactive nature that furniture and art share.

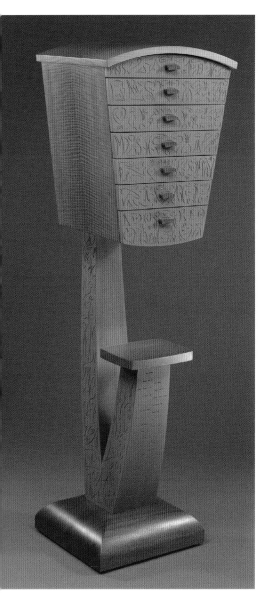

"Aaron's Table and Chairs." Extension table for playing board games. Morse code carved on chair backs reads: "Let the games begin." Bubinga, curly maple, Italian poplar, basswood, milk paint, and upholstery. 48" x 30" x 36". *Courtesy of Clements/Howcroft.*

"Adornment," jewelry stand. Figured makore, mahogany, carved and painted basswood, cherry, fabric, milk paint, and varnish. 18" x 57" x 16". 2007. *Courtesy of Clements/Howcroft.*

"Coffee Table." Bird's eye maple, bubinga, incise carved and milk painted basswood, varnish. 40" x 18" x 18". 2010. *Courtesy of Clements/Howcroft.*

"Blue/Green Console." Cherry, incise carved and painted basswood, glass shelves, milk paint, lacquer. 54" x 36" x 18". 2007. *Courtesy of Clements/Howcroft.*

"Queen Anne Lowboy." Solid mahogany. 35" x 31" x 21". 2009.

Moriah Doucette & Matthew Wolfe

Center Conway, New Hampshire

Furniture making is an art form with endless possibilities. There is so much to know and learn that it can be a lifelong endeavor in which you can always challenge your current skills. The feeling of "limitlessness" is one of the things that drew us both to furniture making. It is rewarding to turn a rough piece of lumber into a beautiful, functional piece of furniture that will be used and enjoyed for generations.

We believe in using time tested techniques and joinery throughout all of our furniture, the same that can be found on fine antiques that are still around and functional today. This ensures that our furniture will stand the test of time and become the antiques of tomorrow. We take pride in hand selecting the highest quality hardwoods for each piece of furniture we make. Whether we're using wide, richly colored cherry, heavily figured tiger maple, amazing walnut, or mahogany, we pay close attention to matching grain, figure, and color. In most cases, all the wood for one project will be cut from the same tree.

Being custom furniture makers, we are able to work in a variety of styles. We've built antique reproductions, period inspired pieces, and custom designed contemporary pieces. Nothing compares to the satisfaction we feel when we finally see the completed piece in a clients home. We look forward to working with new and interesting clients, designing and handcrafting a piece of furniture that combines both function and aesthetics.

"Desk and Bookcase." Solid cherry. 88" x 40" x 22". 2012.

"Sheraton Style Nightstands."
Solid mahogany with turned legs.
19" x 28" x 16". 2011.

"Slant Top Desk on Frame."
Solid mahogany and cherry.
34" x 41" x 18". 2011.

"Reproduction Newport Chippendale Corner Chairs." Solid genuine mahogany with Italian
leather slip seat. 29.5" x 30.5" x 27.5". 2011. These chairs are reproductions of chairs
made by John Goddard of Newport, Rhode Island, in 1760 for Nicholas and John Brown.

John Reed Fox

Acton, Massachusetts

I n 1981, I traveled to Japan. I had been working as a furniture maker for a couple of years and was already using, or trying to learn to use Japanese hand tools. The visit provided me with the opportunity to contemplate and better appreciate the role of the handmade object in a setting where it was a vital part of the culture rather than the anachronism that it was here at home. I was deeply moved by the reverence for materials and process in the traditional architecture, gardening, woodworking, tool making, and other crafts. While I had always been attracted aesthetically to the "simple," it was there that I began to understand how truly rich and deeply informed the "simple" could be.

So now I find that I've been designing and building one-of-a-kind furniture for more than thirty years. Throughout that time, this quotation from Soetsu Yanagi has been my guide: "Beyond all question of old or new, the human hand is the ever-present tool of human feeling…Young people nowadays judge according to whether a piece is new or old, but more important is whether it is true or false." My goal is furniture that finds its balance at the intersection of craftsmanship, material, and design. My pieces represent the accumulation of my skills, sensibility, and understanding and hopefully the development of a mature, authentic voice that informs my effort to create functional, decorative, elegant furniture.

I work in solid wood or hand-sawn veneers. I work primarily premium grade North American hard and soft woods to hand planed or spoke shaved surfaces, which are finished with oil or shellac or in some cases left unfinished.

"Jasmine Cabinet." Cherry and East Indian rosewood. 24" x 54" x 15".

"Donna's Cabinet." Cherry and Port Oreford cedar, and paper. 39.5" x 32" x 15.5".

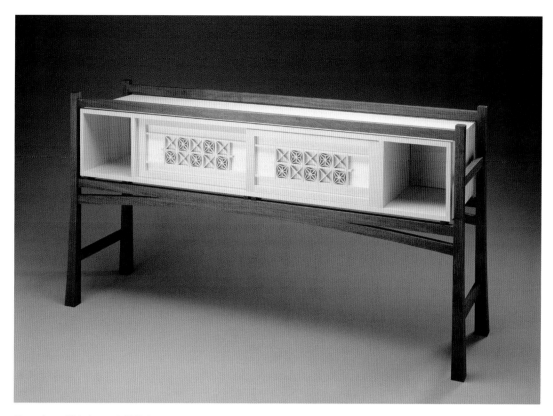

"Lueders Sideboard." Walnut, Alaskan yellow cedar, and handmade paper. 66.5" x 32" x 17".

Detail showing "asa no hana."

"Tall Tansu Dresser." Cherry, East Indian rosewood, maple, and basswood. 38.5" x 50" x 17".

New England

Courtesy of Elizabeth Siler.

Duncan Gowdy

Holden, Massachusetts

"Wall Cabinet with Branches." Ash, white oak, and stain. 22" x 32" x 8". 2009. *Courtesy of Dean Powell.*

I grew up in Needham, Massachusetts, in an area of town that is within walking distance to the Charles River, farming fields, and woodland. The river, the fields, and the woods were my playground. The environment set the stage for the work that I have created within the past seven years. It also instilled in me a sense of place that has influenced where I feel most comfortable: pastoral places where I have lived, including Alstead, New Hampshire, Shelburne, Massachusetts, and now Holden.

My camera has been the main tool for collecting images that connect these places to my work. I walked along a pathway in Shelburne, where pine branches were at eye level. A partially frozen book inspired a graphic image. The swirling Charles River in early spring led to a serene image.

I like to make casework pieces of furniture that serve a useful purpose: blanket chests, wall cabinets, sideboards, and chests of drawers. The clean lines of the forms act as a frame for the imagery. I learned my technique for transferring images to door or drawer fronts in a grade school art class with an opaque projector. Now I use my computer to store photographs. I crop images and project an image before carving and staining it into the wood.

I also have a growing affinity for local wood. I have been able to find wonderful sources for lumber, from the Berkshires to my brother's farm in New Hampshire. Along with having a connection to the images in my furniture, I have a connection to the wood as well, either from knowing where the tree stood or learning from the person who cut the tree and milled the lumber.

"Sideboard with Tidal Image." Ash, quarter-sawn white oak, and stain. 54" x 33" x 17". 2006. *Courtesy of Dean Powell.*

"Charles River Blanket Chest." Maple, ash, and stain. 39" x 21" x 16". 2011. *Courtesy of Dean Powell.*

"Brook Cabinets." Rift-sawn white oak, ash, and stain. 11" x 38" x 8" (each). 2008. *Courtesy of Dean Powell.*

"Dresser with Glacial Shadow." Ash, maple, and stain. 33" x 54" x 17". 2008. *Courtesy of Dean Powell.*

New England

John & Andrea
Hartcorn

Housatonic, Massachusetts

My goal is make the simple line compelling: to strip things down to their barest essentials and still keep it interesting. I like to mix media and different woods together when I can to accept certain lines in my designs.

"Shoshin." Douglas fir. 45" x 34" x 17". *Photo by Lance Patterson.*

"The Japanese Consul." Curly maple and mahogany. 65" x 30" x 16". *Photo by Lance Patterson.*

"The Dragonfly Desk." Cherry with ebony and cherry pulls. 60" x 24" x 33". *Courtesy of Eric Limon Photography.*

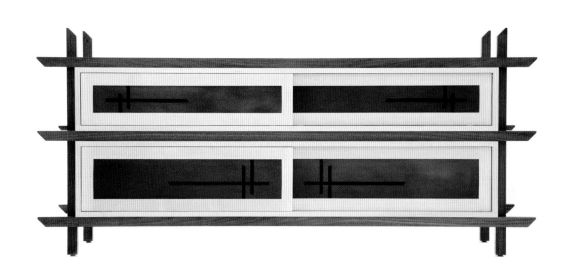

"The Glass Sticks." Maple and walnut with sandblasted glass panels. 65" x 28" x 20". *Photo by Eric Limon.*

"Cherrystone Coffee Table." Cherry and marble. 40" x 16" x 16". *Photo by Lance Patterson.*

New England

John Herbert

Boston, Massachusetts

"Ballerina, Side Tables." Mahogany, curly maple, paint, and copper. 21" x 17". *Courtesy of Matthew Wynne.*

I am lucky. Every day, I have the opportunity to design and create unique and beautiful furniture for my clients. My style continues to evolve, and it is exciting to incorporate new materials and textures into my pieces.

One of the things I strive for in my work is to make furniture that appears to "float." Achieving this adds a level of complexity to the creative process that is challenging, but is worth the effort in the end result.

Foremost, I try to have fun with the craft. I want to make unique pieces that will make people happy to have them in their lives. A beautiful and functional design should add joy each time you see it. When asked what my favorite piece is, my answer is always the same: "My favorite piece is the last one I made."

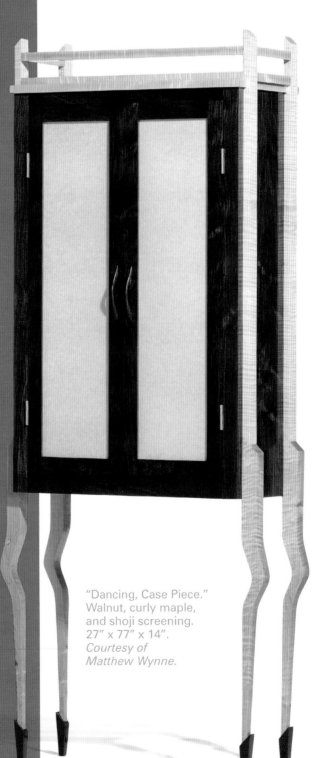

"Dancing, Case Piece." Walnut, curly maple, and shoji screening. 27" x 77" x 14". *Courtesy of Matthew Wynne.*

"WOW, Tall Clock." Cherry, curly maple, paint, copper leaf, brass. 28" x 64" x 16". *Courtesy of Jerome Eno.*

"Floating Coffee Table." Cherry and painted ash. 54" x 19" x 17". *Courtesy of Jerome Eno.*

"Copper Leaf Mirror." Stained ash, paint, and copper leaf blocks. 28" x 70". *Courtesy of | Jerome Eno.*

Silas Kopf

Northampton, Massachusetts

"Bad Hare Day." Macassar ebony, walnut, maple, and marquetry. 58" x 28" x 41". 2008.

I discovered marquetry when I first began making furniture almost forty years ago. I successively encountered French Art Nouveau, Italian Renaissance, Art Deco, and finally classical French furniture. All of these styles relied on marquetry to enhance the design of the piece. My intent is to use the decoration in a modern way, integrating the pictures with the design of the furniture object. My technique is essentially the same as it was two hundred years ago. I start with a furniture concept and then search for a marquetry concept that could work with it. The design bounces back and forth between the three-dimensional design and the decoration, until the satisfactory balance is reached. If I can add a bit of a humorous twist, so much the better.

My intent is to make furniture with very high craft standards, always with an eye to the object's functionality. Most of my marquetry is made of wood, but occasionally I will add metal, shell, or stone. The years of making marquetry haven't diminished my enthusiasm. It's still exciting to stand back and see a finished piece of furniture. And yet I always ask myself, "What would I do differently if I were to make this again?"

"Aloha Shirt Cabinet." Maple, bird's eye maple, and marquetry. 64" x 22" x 17". 2009.

"Three Mile Island" desk and chair. Pommele sapele, machiche, satinwood, and mother-of-pearl. 60" x 28" x 30". 2006.

"Aquarium Blanket Chest." Marquetry: wood, brass, mother-of-pearl, and stone. 38" x 47" x 16". 2011.

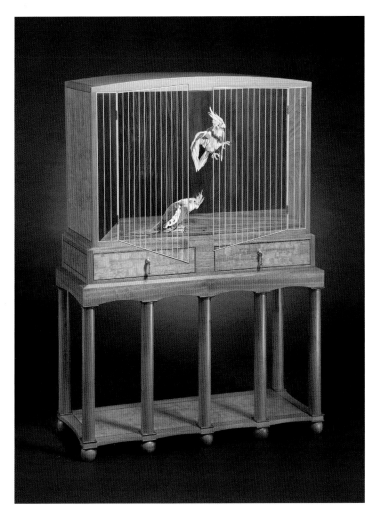

"Jailbreak." Mahogany and marquetry. 54" x 47" x 16". 2008.

"School Desk." Maple, curly maple, walnut, and marquetry. 60" x 30" x 30". 1991.

New England

Dave LeBleu
Westford, Massachusetts

Growing up as the son of a carpenter, working with wood has always been part of my life. I was pressed into action helping my father with various projects from the time I was six or seven. From building my first crude workbench at age 14 to doing finish carpentry on my own home, woodworking is in my blood. I became curious about creating furniture in my early twenties. I am a professional musician and while performing on the road in 1985, I discovered a local cabinetmaker with a beautiful array of furniture. After several visits to his showroom, I was inspired to join the creative art of designing and building furniture. I am primarily self-educated. *Fine WoodWorking* magazine has been an invaluable reference, which I read from cover to cover every month. I've benefitted from taking a few design classes and most especially by being a member of Eastern Massachusetts Guild of Woodworkers. The Guild allows me to gain knowledge from furniture makers of whom I have the utmost regard.

When designing a new piece, I spend quite a bit of time researching, sketching, and paying careful attention to the final dimensions of my creation. Every piece is unique and very much a labor of love. I must admit, I have a tough time parting with each one. I've built pieces ranging from a pulpit for my local church to a standing lamp that features a 12" spider holding the bulb to built in cabinets, among other pieces of furniture.

"Franklin Pillow Platform Bed." Solid walnut and three-part wipe on finish with wax. Headboard detail of pillow shape. *Courtesy of John Connell III.*

"Cherry Rocker and Side Table." Cherry, mahogany, and walnut. *Courtesy of John Connell III.*

"Six-Drawer Dresser." Maple with cherry drawers, three-part wipe on finish for carcass, and drawers with polyurethane tops. *Courtesy of John Connell III.*

"Cherry Dining Table with Cherry and Ash Dining Chairs." Three-part wipe on finish with wax. *Courtesy of John Connell III.*

New England

Timothy Philbrick

Narragansett, Rhode Island

"Grecian Sofa" with loose cushion. Curly soft maple, silk fabric, fringe, and tassels. 66" x 32" x 24". 1985.

*T*he Shorter Oxford English Dictionary defines proportions as "the relation of one part to another." Pleasing proportions render the whole harmonious, symmetrical, and agreeable. I feel that this is central to good furniture design.

With considered, but rough, mathematical proportions arrived at visually, I strive to create furniture which is graceful, balanced, and sensuous. I try to give each piece a clear, quietly stylish stance. Finally, I attempt to select woods that complement the overall feel of a piece and grain patterns that enhance the curve or shape of an individual part.

"Palissandre." East Indian rosewood with satinwood interior bench with calfskin seat. Steinway & Sons Model "B". 2000. *Courtesy of Steinway and Sons.*

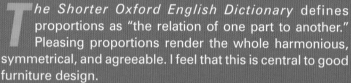

"Sideboard." Claro walnut with satinwood pulls and inlay. 40" x 70" x 20". 1992. *Courtesy of RicMurray Studio.*

Courtesy of Beau Jones/IDC.

"Secretary." Cuban and Honduras mahogany. 44" x 98" x 24".
2003. *Courtesy of Karenphilippi.com.*

New England

Jodi Robbins
Cambridge, Massachusetts

"Curvy Leg Table." Figured maple. 19" x 32" x 10". *Courtesy of Half Crown Design & William Henry Furniture.*

I believe in timeless design, simplicity of line, perfect proportion, and the unique beauty of the material. My pieces are generally unadorned, their lines drawing on timeless classics influenced by early American and mid-century furniture. I also adore the graceful curves of classic French, the unapologetic glamour of Art Deco, and the coyness of Art Nouveau periods as well. I find inspiration all around me and in the least expected places. I am a gatherer of imagery, I take pictures, tear magazine pages out, and sketch to record a moment for future building blocks of design.

I also listen. I have long conversations with my clients about not only furniture but other areas of life as well. I listen to people's needs and wants, learn about what they are passionate about and attracted to, and then take all of that information and distill it into a design that will meet their needs for years to come.

I love the relationships that I have built with my clients over the years and in my local community as well. I feel fortunate to be able to work at something that I am so passionate about and to be embraced by a community that appreciates my eye and my craft.

"Live Edge Coffee Table." Slab walnut with a stained mahogany base. 30" x 18" x 50". *Courtesy of Half Crown Design & William Henry Furniture.*

"Sofa" with custom upholstery.
78" x 32" x 34". *Courtesy of
Half Crown Design &
William Henry Furniture.*

"Modern Console." Walnut.
84" x 26" x 18". *Courtesy of
Half Crown Design &
William Henry Furniture.*

"Danish Modern Table."
Slab walnut and stained mahogany.
42" x 30" x 72". *Courtesy of Half
Crown Design & William
Henry Furniture.*

New England

Kevin Rodel

Brunswick, Maine

"Conference Table." Glass top with wenge legs and grid, cypress crossties, and leather and dyed hemp-rope accent details. 88" x 32.5" x 38" (30" to glass top). *Courtesy of Darren Setlow Photography.*

My interest in woodworking began in my early 20s while living in Philadelphia. I had volunteered to do repair and maintenance work on the ship, Gazella Primera, a 180-foot wooden barkentine then owned by the Philadelphia Maritime Museum. Within a few years, I found myself in Maine where most of the ship's "crew" hailed from. I was fortunate to land a job at Thos. Moser Cabinetmakers, then a small but growing company in New Gloucester, Maine.

After several years of learning the skills of traditional joinery and the subtle but celibate details of Shaker design, I was ready for a change. I opened my own shop in 1986 and soon embraced the kaleidoscopic variety of the International Arts & Crafts Movement. Here was a design philosophy born in the chaos of the Industrial Revolution that actively encouraged innovation and adaptation in all areas of design. For the first time in history, Western design was permitted to be sexy! In addition, I was deeply influenced by the exotic allure of Asian designs.

In 2001, I began instructing part-time at the Center for Furniture Craftsmanship in Rockport, Maine. I continue to teach there each year and at other woodworking schools around the country. Teaching is a great way to gain exposure to the ideas and designs of other craftspeople. I also write on the subject and fulfill commissions from of my shop in Brunswick, Maine.

Now, after 25 years of venturing out on my own, I still work hard to infuse a strong sense of the present into my designs without jettisoning those comforting and familiar aspects of traditional forms and materials that link us to our past. I use the highest quality, sustainably harvested hardwoods and frequently incorporate other visual and tactile materials into my designs, such as stained glass, leather, and even rope knot-work, a distant connection to my early days on a tall ship.

"Hoffmann Style End Tables." Accent tables in white oak and cypress. White table is bleached, and black table is ebonized. 20" x 27.5" x 20.5". *Courtesy of Darren Setlow Photography.*

"Glasgow Desk." Cherry writing desk with leaded-glass inserts in leg recesses and inlaid top. The detail views the glass leg inserts and inlaid top. 72" x 30" x 32". *Courtesy of Darren Setlow Photography.*

"Ikebana Table." Glass top display table in ebonized cherry and cypress with leaded-glass inserts in leg recesses. Detail shows "jin-di-sugi" surface treatment as well as joinery that are visible through the glass top. 82" x 28" x 20". *Courtesy of Dennis Griggs Tannery Hill Studio's, Inc.*

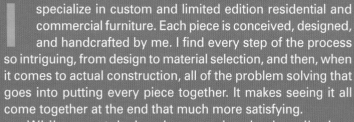

Photo by Thaddeus B. Kubis, copyright 2010.

Jo Ruskin Roessler

Easthampton, Massachusetts

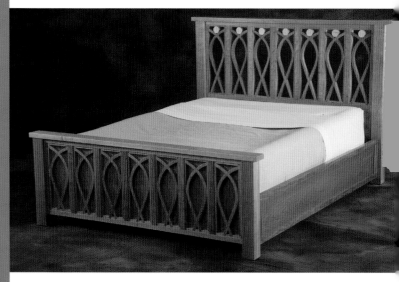

"Elaine's Bed." Cherry and bird's eye maple. My first foray into designing with curves was inspired by a detail on a serving plate designed by Frank Lloyd Wright.

I specialize in custom and limited edition residential and commercial furniture. Each piece is conceived, designed, and handcrafted by me. I find every step of the process so intriguing, from design to material selection, and then, when it comes to actual construction, all of the problem solving that goes into putting every piece together. It makes seeing it all come together at the end that much more satisfying.

While my style has been variously described as "modern," "architectural," and "Japanese-influenced," I eschew such neat categorizations of my work. I don't have a rule book or dogma about adhering to one particular style and take my cues from everyday objects, nature, the world around me, something as basic as a leaf – simplicity and elegance on the surface, but with an amazing underlying complexity.

For over eighteen years, I have been designing under the moniker of Nojo Design. My work is exhibited at prestigious and juried design and craft shows throughout the eastern United States. I have been featured on Home and Garden television and written up in numerous books and periodicals.

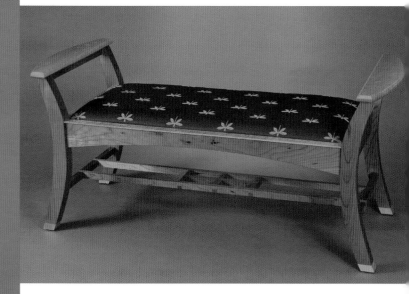

"Nojo Upholstered Bench." Cherry and bird's eye maple.

"M Series Side Tables." Walnut and koa.

"M Series Bed." Walnut and koa.

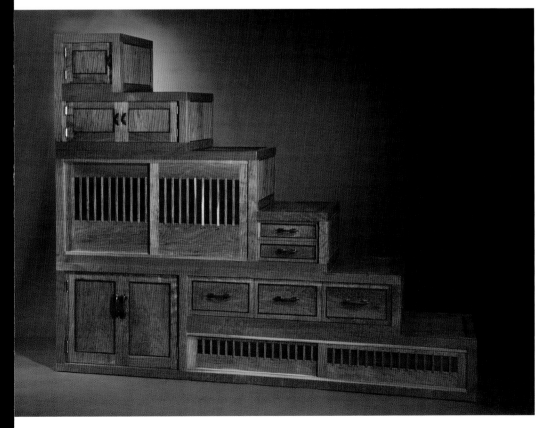

"Tucker Stepped Cabinet." Cherry and walnut.
My first stepped cabinet, a modern take on
traditional Tansu cabinets.

New England

Jules Siegel
Lexington, Massachusetts

I was trained as a mechanical engineer spending most of my career in the aerospace industry concerned with long-range ballistic missiles. In retirement, I turned my lifelong interest in woodworking into a serious hobby focused on designing and constructing unique, useful, and beautiful furniture for my home.

In terms of style, I believe my designs represent an attempt to achieve a feeling of lightness and simplicity, while incorporating construction complexities that assure strength and longevity and which will be appreciated by cognoscenti. Some designs are accented by the incorporation of display details (wood/tiles/drawer pulls), which were collected during travels to Africa and Peru. Some pieces incorporate painted sections to enhance the contrast with natural wood. My wife, Carol, serves as a wonderful sounding board during the design process and then with final tweaking of details.

My training is primarily based on self teaching, but I have taken a number of short courses at the North Bennet Street School in Boston. I am an active participant in the Woodworkers Guild of the Lexington Arts & Crafts Society and The Eastern Massachusetts Guild of Woodworkers.

"Chest on Chest." Cherry cases, box joints with walnut inserts, walnut cock beading on cherry drawer fronts, walnut stand, and painted aluminum drawer pulls. 60" x 18" x 17". *Courtesy of D. Peter Lund.*

"Reference Book Stand." Cherry, African Ebony inlays. 32" x 22" x 30". *Courtesy of D. Peter Lund.*

"Peruvian Chest." Cherry case, doorframes, and drawer fronts; painted poplar panels; hand-made Peruvian tile inserts; and bronze drawer pulls. *Courtesy of D. Peter Lund.*

"Decorative Hall Table." Cherry, and hand blown multi colored glass inserts. *Courtesy of D. Peter Lund.*

Cheval Mirror. Teak and beveled edge mirror. 60" x 27" x 21". *Courtesy of D. Peter Lund.*

Thomas Throop

New Canaan, Connecticut

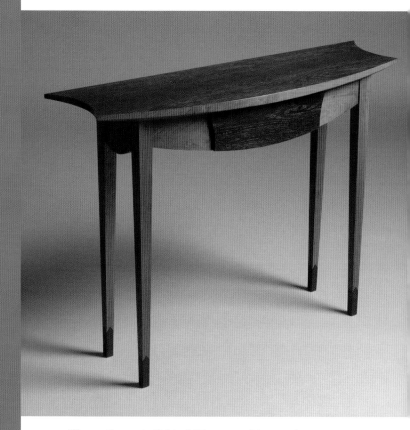

"Essex Console Table." Cherry and bog oak. 44" x 32" x 13".

The smell, the color, the texture, the grain pattern – for as long as I can remember, I have always been passionate about wood and making things with it. Furniture seemed an inevitable way to embrace that passion. My training in England at The John Makepeace School lent structure to this idea in both creative and practical ways. I came to understand that designing and making furniture is not only a means to problem solving but also a form of expression. That expression is rooted at the intersection of design, function, material, and craft. It incorporates my clients' needs. It reflects part of my character.

Most of the furniture I make is done to commission. Although the pieces vary – desks, beds, cabinets, benches, and the like – the one constant among all of these forms is the harmony of design, craft, and material. The making process depends on these elements coming together as a whole. Rich woods, subtle details, and elegant design inform aesthetics and function. Finding the zone where these essentials come into perfect proportion is challenging, occasionally frustrating, and ultimately rewarding.

"Cunard Sideboard." Oregon walnut, English elm burl, white oak and bog oak. 72" x 36" x 19".

"Camden Cabinet." Oregon walnut, hand-rived slate, and bog oak. 39" x 36" x 18".

"Durham Cabinet." Cherry and English pippy elm. 32" x 47" x 17".

"Howard Desk" detail. Mahogany, redwood burl, and walnut. 51" x 37" x 26".

New England

Peter S. Turner

South Portland, Maine

Early on, I came up with this summation of what I do: I work to commission, designing and building contemporary, hardwood furniture. Tradition enters through the forms, joinery, and care that shape my process. I build pieces that I love with the aim that they, in turn, find others who share this feeling. My goal is that every piece precisely meets the needs and desires of each client in a form that uplifts.

Probably about a quarter of the CDs in my shop are circa 1972, my last year of high school. Like my musical preferences, the forms and proportions that I favor often float in from my past. This piece grew out of sketches made while designing an earlier box on bench. The green, poplar box for this earlier piece had served as a photo prop used to illustrate a mitering technique in my recent book on blanket chests. The book had sprouted from a blanket chest I had made for an article in Fine Woodworking magazine from two years ago. One thing has clearly led to another.

Twenty-three years ago, my hands told me that I needed to start working wood. My dad had made shelves for the house, and I remembered being with him while he worked in his small, basement shop. That may have been the seed, but working with my hands was and still is my motivation. Now, with each piece, I try to incorporate something new, something I haven't done before. A technique, a new form, a new material, each one allows me to keep learning. This keeps me engaged and gives life to my work.

"Arrow Rocker." Rift sawn white oak, paper cord, tung oil, and shellac. 23" x 32.5" x 17.5". 2007. *Courtesy of Dennis Griggs.*

"Listening Bench." Maple, blistered maple (rungs), fabric, and wipe-on poly. 60" x 18" x 17.5". 2011. *Courtesy of Dennis Griggs.*

"Ryan Trestle Table." Blistered maple, curly maple, ebony (wedges), and wipe-on poly. 96" x 29" x 36". 2008. *Courtesy of Dennis Griggs*.

"Closed Hutch," opened. Cherry, bird's eye maple, quarter sawn maple, and wipe-on poly. 36" x 76" x 20". 2007. *Courtesy of Dennis Griggs*.

"Bowling Bench." Ash, shagbark hickory, Macassar ebony, paper cord, wipe-on poly, and shellac (seat). 63" x 19" x 18". 2006. *Courtesy of Bill Truslow*.

Seth Walter

South Windsor, Connecticut

I create pieces that bring together all the elements of great furniture that people crave for their surroundings. Natural live edges on gorgeous slabs of wood, traditional styles that people are comfortable with, and structured industrial forms that call out a feeling of strength combine to bring balance and harmony to functional pieces of furniture.

As a furniture and cabinetmaker, I want to impress people with my work. Wood is a beautiful medium, and most of the furniture that people see in stores is unimpressive, mass-manufactured brown or white pieces that look a lot like everything else they have seen: cheap, utilitarian, and unfulfilling. I like to combine contrasting woods and use geometric shapes to create unique, artful pieces of furniture. I want my work to display an appreciation for the grain and quality of the wood itself, while maintaining an expert level of craftsmanship.

I believe a person's furniture says a lot about who they are and how they want to live. It needs to fit the space while simultaneously standing out for its attractiveness. I don't want it to scream out "look at me!" but, instead, be the poised beauty that everyone notices. My goal when working with a client is to deliver all of those points. I provide them with pieces of furniture that they love to have for the rest of their lives. I want my work to be something that enriches the life of whoever sees it, whoever inquisitively feels the surface, and whoever contemplates the beauty, structure, and craftsmanship involved.

"Above the Flame." Walnut and flamed copper veneer. 26" x 17" x 25". 2010. *Courtesy of Maurice DeLage.*

"Wine Table." Walnut, maple, and cherry. 42" x 20" x 36". 2008. *Courtesy of Maurice DeLage.*

"Kusabi." Cherry and ebonized white oak. 45" x 17" x 19.8". 2008.
Courtesy of Maurice DeLage.

"Focus Table." Curly ash and walnut veneer.
19" x 19" x 32". 2010.
Courtesy of Maurice DeLage.

"Bamboo Coffee Table." Bamboo, steel, and walnut. 40" x 21" x 17". 2009.
Courtesy of Maurice DeLage.

Courtesy of Julee Holcombe.

Leah Woods

Portsmouth, New Hampshire

"Coffee Table." Dyed walnut and glass. 64" x 52" x 29". 2010. *Courtesy of Bear Kirkpatrick.*

B y exploring and experimenting in my design process, I am able to push the boundaries of what defines a piece of furniture or a functional object. Technique, material, form, and size are the loose categories within which I work and that allow me to investigate what an object can communicate or offer to a viewer. I am inspired to make work that ranges on the spectrum from emphasizing function to expressing sculptural form.

Objects that offer a more generic function, such as tables, allow me to think about simplicity, asymmetry, line, and space. In contrast, objects that offer a more specific function, such as cabinets, help me to direct my design process and narrow my parameters. Cabinets for shoes, jewelry, or lingerie, as examples, offer me the opportunity to think about small spaces, color, accessibility, and display.

Wood has been my material of choice, whether building functional furniture or sculptural forms. The warmth of the material and its range of emotion from rough and weathered, when the material is left natural, to soft and silky, by shaping and sanding, provide an endless array of options to explore.

"Hall Table." Maple and white oak. 58" x 16" x 38". 2008. *Truslow Photo.com.*

"The Perfect Pair: A Cabinet for Shoes and their Corresponding Handbag." 16" x 11" x 73". 2008. *Truslow Photo.com*

"Bespoke: A Cabinet for a Gentleman's Shoes." White oak, dye, stainless steel hardware. 51" x 18" x 42". 2009. *Courtesy of Dean Powell Photography.*

Yoko Zeltserman-Miyaji

Medford, Massachusetts

I have a deep connection with the materials with which I work – wood and urushi (Japanese lacquer). It is my acceptance of the characteristics of these materials that drives and informs my work.

I moved to America in 2004. I realized that my pieces were different from studio furniture being made here. My woodworking techniques, joinery, and urushi finishing were all different. And so I came to make my Butsudan series. Standing outside of my culture, I went back to it in a way that I couldn't when I was in Japan. I took elements from my culture – both past and present – Butsudan, roadside shrines, and anime, and came up with the series. While working on this series, I developed a part of me that I had not developed before. My other work is also part of me.

Years ago, when I was a student at the Kyoto City University of Art, I saw a slide lecture containing images of American studio furniture. I was amazed and smitten. The concept of furniture as sculpture was entirely new to me – I had not seen anything like it in Japan. I changed my major from maki-e ("painting" with urushi) to woodworking. I've come full circle, showing my work in America where it all began for me.

"Butsudan I ro ha." Mahogany, clear urushi, black urushi, color pigment (green, red, white), and urushi powder. 21" x 18" x 10.5". 2008. *Photo courtesy of Mobilia Gallery.*

"In Balance 2." Mahogany, MDF, clear urushi, cashew paint, black lacquer, and gold leaf. 67" x 32" x 9". 2010. *Photo by Dean Powell Photography.*

"In Balance 1." White oak, black urushi, clear urushi, cashew paint, and polyurethane. 71" x 35" x 8.75". 2003. *Museum of Arts & Design NY. Gift of the artist. Courtesy of Ed Watkins Photography.*

"Tsugaru Deco." Mahogany, MDF, Clear urushi, urushi with carbon pigment. 63" x 36" x 9". 2011. *Dean Powell Photography.*

2 The Mid-Atlantic States

Courtesy of Sara Rychtarik.

Michael Daniel

Long Island City, New York

"Rusty Board Table." Rusted steel top with polished steel legs. 23.75" x 59.5" x 14.5". 2005. *Courtesy of Tim Dalal.*

I took a rather indirect route to metal sculpting and furniture design. Several years ago, when I was living in Chicago, I started taking found objects like metal shopping carts and old tractor seats and transforming them into functional pieces. The tractor seat barstool, which I have refined and modified over the years, is one of my first designs from this period.

After creating these found object pieces, I knew I wanted to work with metal, but I didn't have the background; I didn't know how to weld. In 1992, I moved to New York and took a metal sculpting class. During that first class, I knew that metal sculpting and design was what I wanted to do for the rest of my life. I spent the next few years teaching myself the craft and developing my own style and technique. I began working full time as a metal designer and sculptor in 1996.

Not many people use only metal in furniture making. Although I use various materials that complement metal, such as glass and wood, I always try to use as much metal as possible. Some people think metal is a cold and sterile material, but I find it to be quite the opposite. Metal can be very warm and beautiful depending on how you treat or patina it.

Of all the objects that I design and create, I find that I am most passionate about making furniture. Furniture has the power to transform a space, and I enjoy seeing how my work alters different environments. When I create a piece of furniture I envision it in the space in which it will reside, and I marvel at the idea that what I have designed will outlast me.

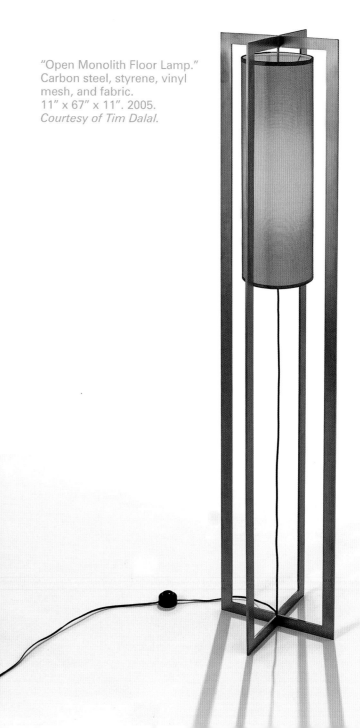

"Open Monolith Floor Lamp." Carbon steel, styrene, vinyl mesh, and fabric. 11" x 67" x 11". 2005. *Courtesy of Tim Dalal.*

"Ceruse Dining Table." Ceruse finished ash with blackened steel legs. 34" x 76" x 30". 2011. *Courtesy of Sara Rychtarik.*

"Tractor Seat Barstools." Recycled tractor seats. Steel bases with adjustable swivel seats. 17" x 25" x 19"; 38" height adjustable. 2005. *Courtesy of Tim Dalal.*

"Sliding Steel and Plexiglas Panels." Orbital sanded steel with frosted plexiglas. Custom sizes. 2000. *Courtesy of Tim Dalal.*

The Mid-Atlantic

Courtesy of Stephen Amiaga.

David N. Ebner

Brookhaven, New York

"Chest of Drawers." Sapele. 33" x 44" x 22".
Courtesy of Stephen Amiaga.

I was born in 1945 and grew up in Buffalo, New York. I was educated at the school for American Craftsmen at Rochester Institute of Technology and studied with furniture craftsman luminary Wendell Castle and also trained at the London School of Furniture Design. My studio is in the hamlet of Brookhaven, on Long Island's south shore, where I have lived since 1973.

My works are in the collections of the Smithsonian American Art Museum, American Craft Museum, and Yale University Art Gallery, among others, as well as numerous private and corporate collections. My work has been featured in a number of prestigious publications, including *Arts and Crafts International, Art & Antiques, Fine Woodworking,* and the *New York Times*.

I approach my art intuitively as well as intellectually, drawing inspiration whenever I find it. I've explored a variety of directions and themes over the years, but each piece is treated as an art object with concern for my material and honesty to its inherent qualities. For me, one's creative ability is demonstrated in the diversity of the pieces and what one learns from change.

"Bench." Cast bronze. 36"
x 17" x 15.5". *Courtesy of
Stephen Amiaga.*

"Library Steps." Walnut. 19" x 49" x 22".
Courtesy of Stephen Amiaga.

"Oval Dining Table," composite detail. Walnut. 54" x 29" x 96".
Courtesy of Stephen Amiaga.

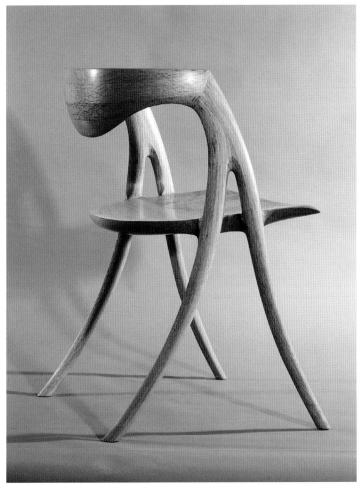

"Writing Chair." Red oak. 20" x 30" x 20".
Courtesy of Stephen Amiaga.

"Onion Chest." Red oak with bleached and painted ash detail.
30" x 44". *Courtesy of Stephen Amiaga.*

S.D. Feather

Bethlehem, Pennsylvania

"Orb Wine Rack." Holds 9 bottles. Steel and textured bronze powder coat. 18" x 12" x 12". 2009. *Photo by 110 Front Communications.*

I started designing furniture about ten years ago as a natural evolution of my talents in graphic design and carpentry. I describe my designs as functional artwork, and not just pieces of furniture. Each piece is intended to be a conversation piece and the focal point of any room.

My furniture designs are heavily influenced by industrial design and futuristic themes, often meshing classic design elements with modern influences. I have designed custom pieces for minor league baseball teams, Fortune 500 companies, as well as one-of-a- kind pieces for clients in Tokyo.

Most recently, I have begun to design pieces influenced by one of my other passions in life, bicycling. For as long as I can remember, I have spent many hours a week on a bike – training, racing, or just biking for pleasure. About two years ago, I started to see how bicycle parts could be incorporated into my designs. This has created an outlet for a new approach to my functional art style. An added benefit to these designs is that I am now able to contribute to the green movement in reclaiming the bicycle parts for new uses.

Ultimately, I just get excited every time I see one of my designs come to life.

"Po Chair." Steel, mirror silver powder coat, and black ultra suede cushion. 24" x 56" x 24". 2001. *Photo by 110 Front Communications.*

"Freestyle Coffee Table." Aluminum and bicycle parts, candy blue powder coat, 0.5" tempered glass top with flat edge. 36" diameter top, 17" tall. 2010. *Photo by 110 Front Communications.*

"Sunflower Wine Rack." 12 bottles. Steel and textured pewter powder coat. 39" x 22" x 12". 2007. *Photo by 110 Front Communications.*

"Arch Coffee Table." Steel, mirror silver powder coat, 0.5" tempered glass top with 1" bevel edge. 36" x 36" x 17". 2005. *Photo by 110 Front Communications.*

"Sprint Coffee Table." Aluminum and bicycle parts, candy red powder coat, 0.25" tempered glass top with flat edge. 36" diameter top, 17" tall. 2010. *Photo by 110 Front Communications.*

The Mid-Atlantic

Ken and Julie Girardini

Sykesville, Maryland

We are a self-taught husband and wife design team, who have been developing and creating works in steel and mixed media for the past twenty years under the name Girardini Design. Our designs are inventive and functional with a contemporary flair. With our custom work, we always respond to our customer's needs and styles, combining them with our experience and design aesthetic, to create the perfect piece for them.

Our sculptural furniture provides a personal springboard for exploration of ideas and techniques that allow us some experimental fun. We are very proud to be making a living with our hands, our imagination, and our skills.

"Asia Wall Clock." Steel and copper clock. 34" x 12".

"Mondrian Fireplace Surround." Steel fireplace surround with color blocks of copper and bronze patina. Glass doors and mantle. Custom made to fit existing fireplace openings.

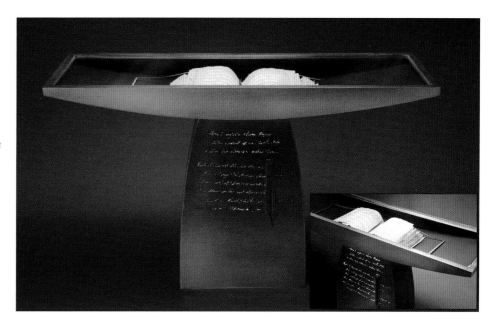

"Written Word Table." Steel, paper, book, and light. 54" x 16" x 34". The "book" below the glass is under lit with glowing words. The base also glows with internally lit script and has a small niche with a blank book for your own famous writings. 2010.

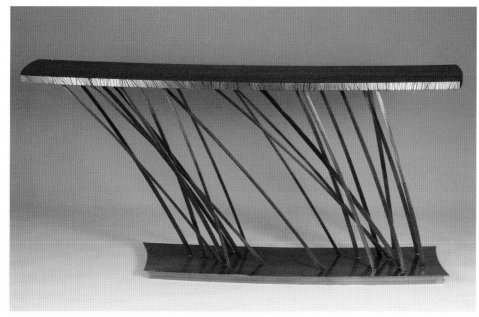

"Brushstrokes Table." One-of-a-kind console table created from solid walnut. The edge has been embellished with copper leaf and carved. A steel base has "brushstrokes" of steel grasses rising from a lake. 72" x 18" x 39". 2009.

Margery E. Goldberg

Washington, D.C.

"Urgan Fire Place." Many exotic woods, neon, and steel. 28" x 26" x 18". *Courtesy of Suzanne Alessi.*

Wood is my love, and I believe I was a tree in my past life. Growing up in Rochester among some of the best woodworkers at Rochester Institute of Technology, I became one of the first female woodworkers in America, able to bring to the medium a sensitivity and concepts that were untried by my male counterparts. Creating full body and fantasy tables wasn't what woodworkers of that day considered.

Machinery became my friend, and I began using a chainsaw and super hog to work with large quantities of wood. I learned early how to stack laminate and turn rough, square, boards of wood into round, sensual, smooth and enticing objects, sculpting figures into tables and desks, adding fantasy and whimsy.

Throughout my career, I've taken large commissions that have changed my direction and stretched my limits and imagination. I started the baseball table series as a commission, and all my desks were commissions. I even created a 16' x 6' x 30" all-walnut conference table that took six people to turn over the top and a crane to move it into the building. I believed that if I could think of it, I could build it. And, I did.

Always one to push boundaries, I also added neon to furniture as a way of altering the environment and changing space with light. Wood is the perfect home for neon; it protects the glass.

Even today, I remain fascinated and inspired by each piece of wood, which lends itself to being unique. I believe trees are our ancestors, and I've named some in my backyard after my relatives.

"Deco Neon Mirror." Purple heart, bird's eye maple, neon, and mirror. 38" x 60" x 4".

"Adam & Eve Desk." Cherry wood and many other exotic woods. 8" x 30" desk ht., 36" front leg ht. x 40" d.

"Earth Mother Cocktail Table." Bubinga and glass with agate eyes. 60" x 20" x 30".

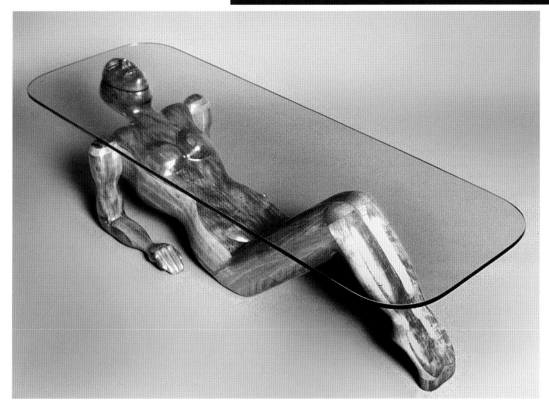

"Pear Body Cocktail Table." Pear wood, cherry wood, and glass. 72" x 17" x 24".

The Mid-Atlantic

Photo by Justin Guarino.

Glen G. Guarino

Cedar Grove, New Jersey

My love for working with wood began when I was nine years old visiting my uncle in England. There, I watched him build a model sailboat. When I returned home, I built a workbench in my parents' basement and started working with simple tools and scrap wood. Over the years, my skills improved, and I began to develop my style. I came to the realization that, if my work were to improve, craftsmanship, material, and function were not enough. The work had to be about form. I decided to earn a fine arts master's degree in studio art.

Now, many commissions later, I hope my furniture conveys a sense of the person behind the art: someone who loves the creative process. Each new design is an adventure, exploring my imagination and the potential of the material. My hands-on approach allows me to let the simplicity of the design reveal itself, creating a piece that imparts serenity and calm, reflecting the tree's grace and strength. As the design becomes real and tangible, I get a sense of a tree evolving into a new life as a useful piece of art. I'm grateful to be the catalyst for this rebirth.

"Allegro." Rescued red oak. 54.25" x 21" x 16". 2008. *Photo by Justin Guarino.*

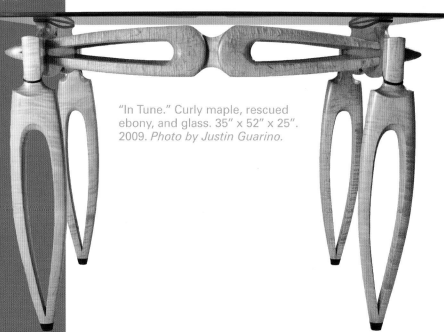

"In Tune." Curly maple, rescued ebony, and glass. 35" x 52" x 25". 2009. *Photo by Justin Guarino.*

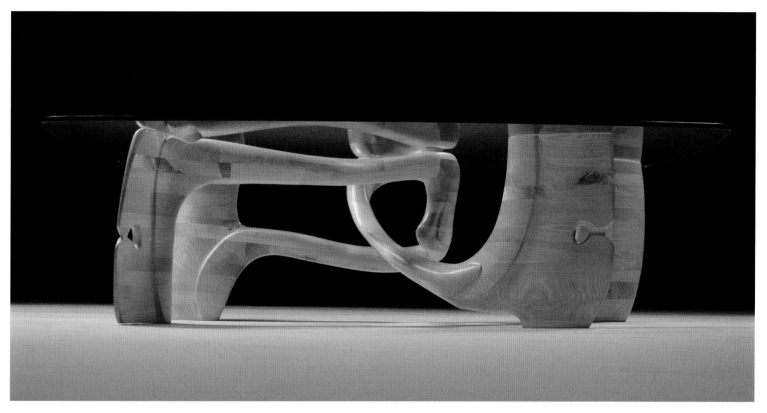

"Coming About." Rescued northern catalpa and glass. 18" x 36" x 68". 2011. *Photo by Justin Guarino.*

"Arabesque." Curly shedua and ebonized sapele.
29.75" x 37.5" x 18". 2009. *Photo by Justin Guarino.*

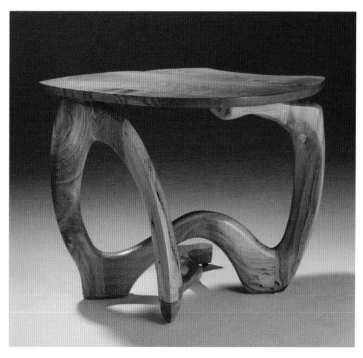

"Storm." Northern catalpa and ash (both rescued).
28" x 37.5" x 29.75". 2020. *Photo by Justin Guarino*

Peter Handler

Philadelphia, Pennsylvania

"Bleached Coral Reef Table." Anodized aluminum, clay (by Karen Singer), bamboo plywood, and glass. 30" x 30". 2011. *Courtesy of Karen Mauch Photography.*

It is my feeling that art should look to the present and the future, rather than to the past, so that the works we create are a statement of our own period and its realities. My furniture is also largely a commissioned body of work. A commission is a leap of faith, and the hope is always that the final work will fulfill the clients' expectations. I take this seriously and always let my clients know how much I value this trust. I want my furniture to give my clients and their families joy in its presence and use. As a maker, one of the things that gives me pleasure is the use of diverse materials. I was a jeweler before I was a furniture maker, so the use of metal (then silver and gold, now aluminum) is a natural for me. Attention to small and hidden details is the primary perspective that I have carried over from my jeweler life. Even if no one else sees them, the client knows they are there. Aluminum is predictable. One of the joys of working with wood is that it is always alive, and no two pieces of wood look alike. I love how wood and colored metal work together.

As an artist in this point in earth's history, I feel compelled to make statements about the state of the world. Furniture is my medium of expression. Talking, visually and verbally, about climate change has become my passion. As an artist, this is one of the things I can do to try to, in my own small way, change the world.

"Empire Coffee Table." Anodized aluminum and curly maple. 54 x 15" x 28". 2005. *Courtesy of Karen Mauch Photography.*

"Bliss Sideboard." Bird's eye maple and anodized aluminum. 54" x 33" x 18". 2005. *Courtesy of Karen Mauch Photography.*

"Caruso Chair." Anodized aluminum, hardwood frame, and velvet. 36" x 39" x 30". *Courtesy of Karen Mauch Photography.*

"Casablanca Chaise." Anodized aluminum, hardwood frame, and silk. 96" x 36" x 30". 2006. *Courtesy of Karen Mauch Photography.*

The Mid-Atlantic

Peter Harrison

Middle Grove, New York

The style of my furniture grew out of a desire to build without traditional woodworking joinery. This began as a method of making furniture, but quickly became integral to the composition and design of my work. I use three materials: wood, metal, and concrete. Each has characteristics that are specifically suited for different elements. The aesthetic nature of the elements long ago became more important than their convenience.

My designs break from traditional furniture forms. It is rare that I build a table with four legs. Decorative components made from stainless steel cables or rods are used as important visual elements. I find these elements give life to my pieces. Pure minimalism errs towards being boring. My work celebrates materials and maintains a pure feeling that is modern without being devoid of details.

It is important to me to create complete pieces. I strive for my furniture to entice the viewer from across the room and captivate them upon closer inspection. Designs must be bold and details crisp. This is a combination of design and craftsmanship. My furniture is openly constructed with exposed fasteners. The heads of stainless steel screws get polished and used as details. They are a view of exposed structure, yet not a complete vision. It is intended as a glimpse of what is inside, a celebration of the beauty of structure rather than a moment of too much information.

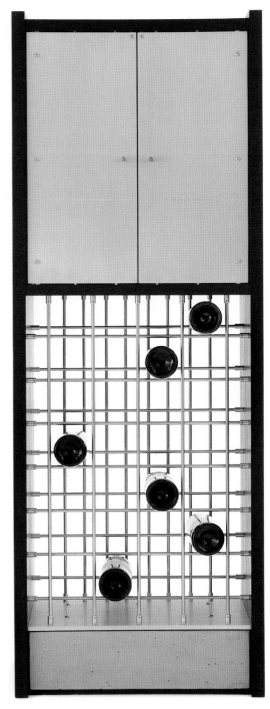

"Infinity." Mahogany dyed black, stainless steel, aluminum, concrete, and glass. 22" x 60" x 12". 2011. *Courtesy of StockStudiosPhotography.com.*

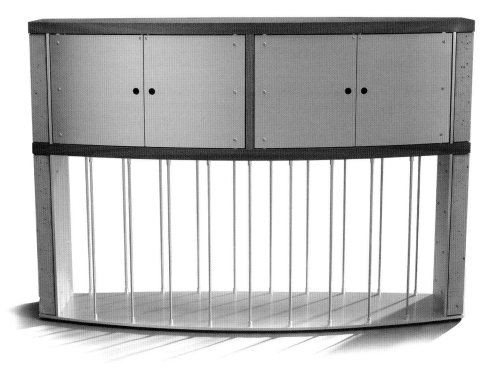

"Tangent." Mahogany, stainless steel, aluminum, and concrete. 60" x 42" x 12". 2008. *Courtesy of StockStudiosPhotography.com.*

"Barossa" wine rack. Mahogany dyed black, stainless steel, and concrete. 9.5" x 63" x 9". 2010. *Courtesy of StockStudiosPhotography.com.*

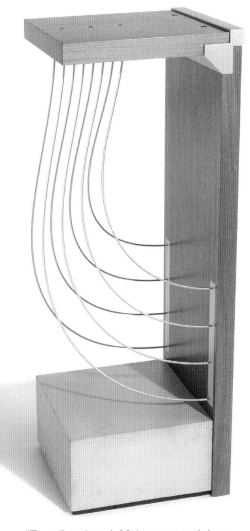

"Torus" pedestal. Mahogany, stainless steel cable, aluminum, and concrete. 12" x 36" x 13". 2010. *Courtesy of StockStudiosPhotography.com.*

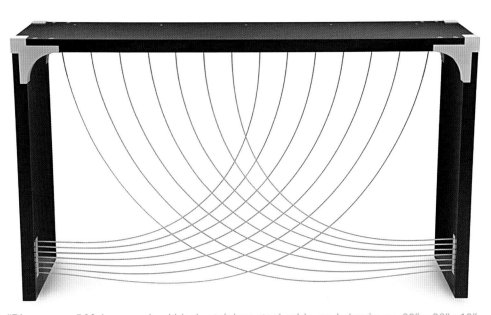

"Divergence." Mahogany dyed black, stainless steel cable, and aluminum. 60" x 36" x12". 2011. *Courtesy of StockStudiosPhotography.com.*

The Mid-Atlantic

David Hubbard

Silver Spring, Maryland

I am an environmentalist and activist living green. I studied art and writing at the University of Maryland and worked in a local ironworks to support myself in college. My accomplishments include painting, printmaking, and large outdoor sculpture. Making tables is an extension of my sculpture.

Using glass as a table surface enables the viewer to see the base designs. My 2005 stainless steel sculpture Night Boat is the first public sculpture made for Potomac, Maryland. I have had my poetry published in several different publications including Zouch online literary magazine. I have also written over thirty songs for "Sky High Radio," a local rock band. My wife, Marcie, and I just published a new children's environmental adventure book, The Shiny Shell. I love canoeing and snorkeling and prefer to spend my free time in wild places. I believe that our top priority must be to change our civilization's direction toward a green future for our children.

"Dolphin Table." Patinated mild steel and glass. 30" x 36". 2002. *Courtesy of Lee Stalsworth Photography.*

"Sacred Grove Table." Rusted coated steel and glass. *Courtesy of Lee Stalsworth Photography.*

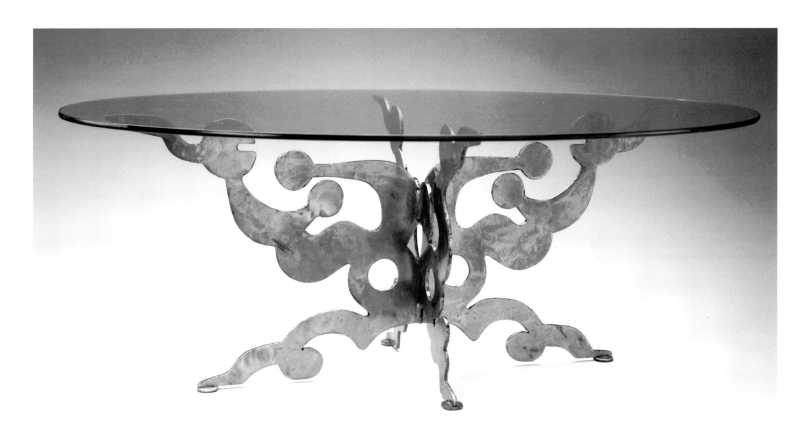

"Trans Coffee Table." Stainless steel and glass. 24" x 24" x 36". 2001. *Courtesy of Lee Stalsworth Photography.*

"Northwest Coast Table." Aluminum and glass. 30" x 36". 2000. *Courtesy of Lee Stalsworth Photography.*

"Conference Table Base." Stainless steel. Base only: 27" x 30" x 42". 2001. *Courtesy of Lee Stalsworth Photography*

The Mid-Atlantic

Paul Malmendier

Lititz, Pennsylvania

"Tannery Three-Sided Coffee Table." Fabricated steel and burnished aged patina. 34" x 20" x 34".

Metalsmithing is a perpetual exchange between the sublime and the base, fluidity and rigidity, give and take. The metal is unyielding, yet when put to flame, it becomes a complacent participant in my creative process, only to muster its toughness again upon quenching. Steel is capable of being fashioned into any form; it can be warm, pleasing, and expressive, and it can be cold, hard, and blank. It is the challenge of understanding this material, and balancing these unique and fascinating qualities that has led me to make metalsmithing my lifelong pursuit. I strive to create pieces that are thoughtful in their design, pleasing to the eye and to the hand, and perfectly suited to their tasks – pieces that embody my vision and spirit, yet remain honest to the nature and temper of the materials from which they are wrought.

"Tannery Sculpted Stool." Fabricated steel and gray/black patina. 16" x 24 (seat height)" x 16". 34" finished height.

"Tannery Credenza." Fabricated steel and plumb brown/black patina. 58" x 26" x 17".

"Floating Top Side Table." Fabricated steel and black patina over copper wash. 17" x 16" x 23".

"Trindle Occasional Table." Fabricated steel and smoky gray patina. 20" x 26" x 20".

"Floating Top Coffee Table." Fabricated steel and smoky gray patina. 40" x 17" x 40".

Andrew Pitts

Heathsville, Virginia

I love to create. I am blessed to make things with my hands and am emotionally involved with my work. I relish the freedom to transform wonderful woods into equally wonderful pieces of art that people can use. Making contemporary hardwood furniture is the most satisfying work I can imagine. My furniture career is a journey where new discoveries are an essential component of the art. The artisan unlocks the wonders of the material, but the synergy of the client/artisan relationship can result in the finest designs, so my client is often my partner in discovery.

Furniture is my art form, my expression of beauty, but my furniture must also be functional. In each piece, I attempt to prove that function and beauty can co-exist harmoniously. I start my designs with the intent of bringing out the natural beauty of the woods, using graceful curvature, exquisitely matching grain patterns, and exacting joinery. Wood is the soul of my furniture. I capture the essence using hardwood logs that grow locally, often giving new life to those that fall in storms, milling and drying the lumber myself to retain the spirit of the wood. I acknowledge the perfection in wood as its imperfection, and I try to use the variations of the material to enhance the beauty of the piece. My carving of fine surfaces allows me to evoke my voice in a way not otherwise possible. I use clear finishes, applied thinly and naturally to avoid masking the figure. The fresh scent of a light shellac polish or the soft texture of an oil and beeswax finish beckons you, connecting you to my work. My work is complete when you discover your personal relationship with the wood and the furniture.

"Shadows of Night Cabinet." Walnut, holly, maple, tulip poplar, ebonized white oak legs, and shellac polish finish. 29" x 63" x 20". 2008.

"Buffet." Curly and quilted maple, cherry with shellac polish and varnish finishes. 60" x 34" x 19". 2011.

"From the Bay." Blanket Chest. Cherry, walnut, tulip polar, cedar lined, ebonized white oak legs, and shellac polish finish. 51" x 36" x 20". 2010.

The Mid-Atlantic

Alex Roskin

Hudson, New York

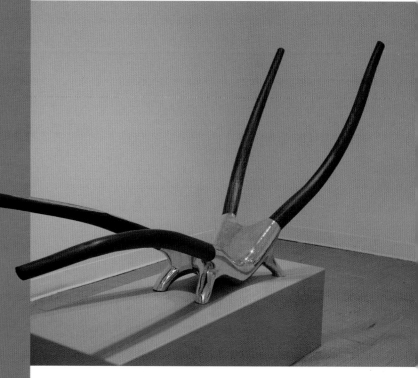

"Tusk Chair." Cocobolo and bronze. 67" x 20" x 34". 2009.

I love to create. I am blessed to make with my hands and am emotionally involved with my work. I relish the freedom to transform wonderful woods into equally wonderful pieces of art that people can use. Making contemporary hardwood furniture is the most satisfying work I can imagine. My furniture career is a journey where new discoveries are an essential component of the art. The artisan unlocks the wonders of the material, but the synergy of the client/artisan relationship can result in the finest designs, so my client is often my partner in discovery.

Furniture is my art form, my expression of beauty, but my furniture must also be functional. In each piece, I attempt to prove that function and beauty can co-exist harmoniously. I start my designs with the intent of bringing out the natural beauty of the woods, using graceful curvature, exquisitely matching grain patterns, and exacting joinery. Wood is the soul of my furniture. I capture the essence using hardwood logs that grow locally, often giving new life to those that fall in storms, milling and drying the lumber myself to retain the spirit of the wood. I acknowledge the perfection in wood as its imperfection, and I try to use the variations of the material to enhance the beauty of the piece. My carving of fine surfaces allows me to evoke my voice in a way not otherwise possible. I use clear finishes, applied thinly and naturally to avoid masking the figure. The fresh scent of a light shellac polish or the soft texture of an oil and beeswax finish beckons you, connecting you to my work. My work is complete when you discover your personal relationship with the wood and the furniture.

Pair of "Skeleton Stools." Rosewood and bronze. One: 16.25" x 28.75" x 28" (41.3 x 73 x 71.1 cm); the other: 17.5" x 28" x 21.25" (44.5 x 71.1 x 54 cm). 2006.

"Skeletal Bench." Rosewood and bronze. 45" x 26" x 23". 2008.

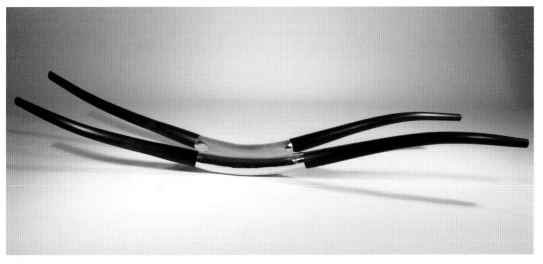

"Tusk Rocker." Rosewood and bronze. 70" x 20" x 18".

Janice Claire Smith

Philadelphia, Pennsylvania

It's wonderful to watch dancers or athletes and see the incredible courage and controlled exuberance they exhibit. I sometimes feel my furniture is like a frozen dance. There is so much action and purpose that goes into it, from daydreaming to brainstorming to drawing, planning, procuring materials, milling, matching grain, cutting parts, cutting joints, sanding, assembling, and finishing. I enjoy them all, except maybe the sanding. Sometimes the work seems almost serene. Other times it feels like I have to wrestle a piece to get it finished. It is labor intensive, but a labor of love. There is fear of flubbing a difficult technique and having to start over. There are experiments trying new techniques that I think will allow me to create the strength and form I am looking for. Finally, there is the satisfaction of finishing a piece and seeing that it matches my idea. I want it to be sculptural but also useful and sturdy. I give my pieces a feeling of movement by using asymmetry and balance. Curves, folds, and acute angles make my furniture lively.

Currently, I design and build furniture in a shop I share with two other woodworkers. I teach woodworking part time at Bucks County Community College and basic carpentry with Philadelphia's Youth Violence Reduction Program with the hope that learning practical skills will empower young adults on probation and parole to start new careers.

"Cathy Lynn Chair." Cherry, African cherry, "Ligna" composite veneer with upholstered seat and back. 29" x 30" x 32". 2005. Ottoman. African cherry, curved plywood, "Ligna" composite veneer, upholstery. 15" x 15" x 17". 2006.

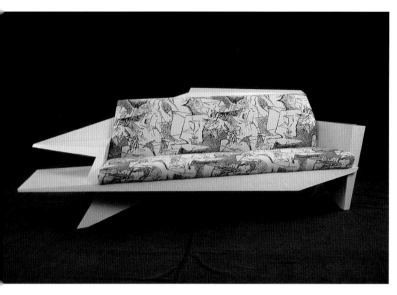

"Origami Couch," front and back. Birch and birch plywood with "Italo Pearl" composite veneer. The double weave fabric by Cynthia Schira was woven on a computerized loom in Germany for this couch. 98" x 31" x 33". 1996.

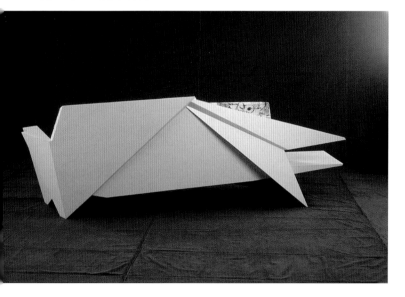

"Whimcycle Chair." Plywood with "Silverlining" composite veneer, painted steel tubing, upholstered seat and back. 53" x 31" x 27". 1995.

The Mid-Atlantic

Fredrick C. Vogt

Richmond, Virginia

I am primarily a furniture and architectural woodwork conservator. In the 1960s, at the age of 16, I began an apprenticeship as a furniture maker during the summer and after school. I continued this through college and into the mid-1970s. I learned the furniture-making trade in a shop that primarily made reproductions of eighteenth and early nineteenth century Continental as well as American furniture. I became enamored with the early maker's styles, choice of materials, proportions, and finishes. In my mid-twenties, I switched my focus to preserving the material that I had been learning to copy for the last decade.

Although I don't focus as much time now on making furniture, I am always thrilled to be commissioned to copy or design a new piece. For over forty years now, my emphasis on classical proportions, hand-made construction, traditional materials, and lustrous, hand-rubbed finishes reflects my classical training and love for the old school methodologies and forms. When requested, I finish my pieces so that it is difficult to tell if they are old or new without looking very closely.

While I appreciate and respect the new ground that modern furniture forms have broken, I don't believe that the evolution of furniture design and construction has eclipsed the combination of strength, gracefulness, functionality, proportion, and beauty so eloquently expressed in the furniture of Thomas Chippendale, Robert Adam, Thomas Sheraton, George Hepplewhite, and others of their genre. While I sometimes make variations on classical themes in my new work, the voices, inspiration, and handwork of the old masters are communicating through the proportions, construction, materials, interplay of light and dark, and polished luster of the finishes on all of the pieces I produce.

"Open Arm Chair." Reproduction of open arm chair by Georges Jacob, Paris, ca. 1785. Thomas Jefferson acquired the original while in Paris; it is now in the collection at Monticello. Solid mahogany with silk brocade upholstery. 24 3/4" x 38 3/8" x 28". *Courtesy of Dennis McWaters.*

"Commode." A piece of my own design and obviously influenced by the style of British furniture designers of the late eighteenth century. The commode departs from tradition with the use of zebra and quilted cherry woods. The balanced layout of these contrasting woods, combined with the more traditional but spectacular satinwood, gives it a powerful presence. The piece is finished with only linseed oil and subdued French polished shellac. The client had requested a specific size for an entrance hall.
58" x 32" x 17". *Courtesy of Katherine Wetzel.*

"Adam Style Folding Card Table." Reproduction of original from a private collection. Solid and veneer flame birch, satinwood veneers, boxwood, and ebonized birch string inlays. 39.25" diameter open; 28.625" tall (overall). *Courtesy of Dennis McWaters.*

John Wesley Williams

Renick, West Virginia

"Seven-Drawer Semainier Chest." Bird's eye maple and ebony. 72" x 20" x 20".

Thirty-five years ago, I had no idea I would spend my life endeavoring to unlock the mystery of why we are so drawn to this material, wood. A few years later, I had the ability to work this material but not to unlock the potential. I was doing about six to eight exhibits a year and was struck by the reaction of viewers as if they were seeing and feeling wood for the first time. The tactile nature of wood when not hidden under layers of plastic finish was immediately discernible by people. Like many furniture makers of my time, I was influenced by Shaker furniture, not its simplicity but its sensibility. Like me, they worked this material more by touch than sight, as I do today.

I started sculpting and shaping my pieces to intensify personal interaction with my work. You had to feel it. That "feel" is the same thing you get from a tool handle that has evolved. The type of sculpting I was doing still allowed the wood to be finished extremely well, which was another component of wood's tactility.

My work has nothing to do with turning wood into the accepted genre of the day or a bygone era. It's a sense of discovery of a material that has been with us forever, but we have forgotten the response it can elicit in us, except when the crafting is handled properly. When a work becomes more of an exploration, it simply excites everything.

"Big Desk." Bird's eye maple and ebony. 72" x 36" x 24".

"Console Case." Cherry, brown bird's eye maple, and inlaid sandstone top. 42" x 36" x 22".

"Dresser." Bird's eye maple and ebony. 42" x 48" x 22".

"Carved Sideboard." Bird's eye maple and ebony. 72" x 36" x 24".

The Mid-Atlantic

Nico Yektai

Sag Harbor, New York

My relationship with furniture predates my technical training at the Rochester Institute of Technology in 1993. I attended the School for American Craft's MFA program in woodworking and furniture design. I grew up making furniture with my father, an abstract expressionist painter. The furniture was not particularly well built, but it did serve as a focal point for discussion about creativity. These lessons were at the core of my development as an artist. I think of myself as a sculptor who makes portraits of furniture. I am trying to capture something more than just a function.

My style evolved to introduce spontaneity into the very static, pre-planned process of making furniture. I looked to the effects of time and use on furniture for a starting point. My style evolved as a pressure cooker of those inevitabilities. I shift boards out of their expected location just like it can happen when they warp or when glue lines fail. I consider these to be the broad movements that help build my pieces up. The components become exceedingly expressive and are at the core of my structural style. I then come back and use facets to soften the edges and balance the asymmetrical composition. Facets evolved from the notion of how an edge gets worn during years of use, again the pressure cooker.

These tools allow me to explore furniture in ways that transcend function. The same piece twice is an impossibility because of decisions that I make at the moment of construction. Two pieces may be similar, but there is endless variation between them. I have been exhibiting my work nationally at art galleries and design shows since opening the doors of my studio in 1995.

"Bench #1" from *Bench Series #2*. Sapele. 81" x 17" x 21".

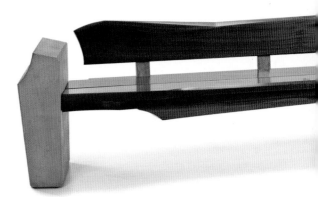

"Bench #4" from *Bench Series #2*.
Sapele, cast concrete, and stainless steel.
117" x 30" x 24".

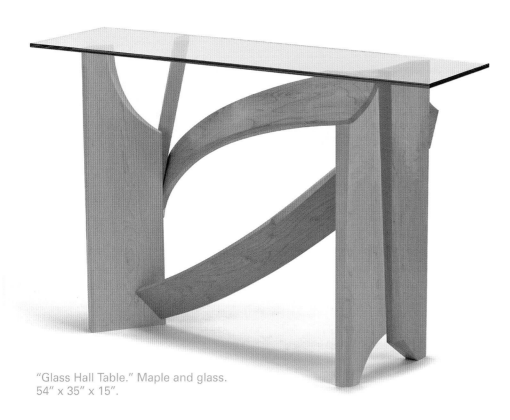

"Glass Hall Table." Maple and glass.
54" x 35" x 15".

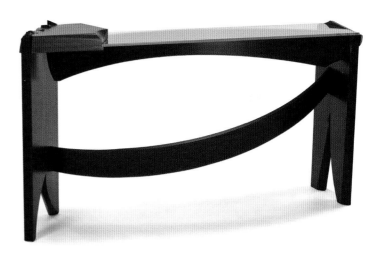

"Curved Dovetail Console Table." Oxidized sapele and glass.
70" x 38" x 15".

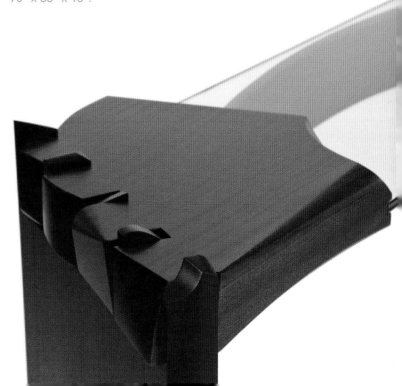

3 The South

The South

Robert Brou

Atlanta, Georgia

I make furniture that I find exciting, full of motion and character: works are carefully composed and complex creations that bring a beautiful piece of nature into your home. My focus is to continue creating designs that explore new forms from the natural world while always producing the finest functional yet sculptural organic furniture possible. I enjoy designing new work.

"Porcupine Coffee Table." Claro walnut, black walnut, and zebrawood. Over 100 zebrawood quills of varying lengths protrude from a mound of black walnut. 23" x 16" x 34". 2008.

"Wave Desk." Poplar and MDF. The two towers are clad in 2.5"-thick poplar lumber carved into a random wave pattern. Between each layer, there is a 0.75" tall reveal, just large enough to fit adult-sized fingers, which eliminates any need for drawer pulls. 24" x 31" x 78". 2010.

"Jellyfish Table." Bubinga (top and base), oak, and acrylic rod. Three acrylic rods that are anchored into an ebonized bubinga base support the bubinga top. Seventy oak tentacles swirl from the top to create a complex visual composition. 21" x 32" x 26". 2009.

"Half Shell Chair."
Black walnut.
27" x 30" x 23". 2011.

"Urchin Coffee Table." Buckeye burl, poplar, and mahogany. A commission based on the design of the original "Urchin" table (2008), this table is smaller than the original with a butterfly cut slab of 1"-thick buckeye burl. Under the top is an ebonized mound of poplar wood with 108 custom-turned mahogany spikes. 22" x 18" x 26". 2011.

The South

Courtesy of Michael Traister

Brian Fireman

Tryon, North Carolina

"Sanctuary Dining Set." Shown with book-matched walnut slabs on top, cherry base, and matching Swallowtail arm chairs and Swallowtail side chairs. The table is 38" x 10" x 30". *Courtesy of Michael Traister.*

The main reason I have chosen to follow the path of designing and building hand-crafted contemporary furniture is that it brings me great joy. Beyond words, I am attracted to the beauty of the material in which I work. In the shop, there are lessons every day. My designs are inspired from many sources, from walks in the woods to overseas travels, but mostly from the wood itself. I equally enjoy working with live-edge slabs, as well as more sculptural work. My intent with both is to allow the inherent beauty of the material to acquire a second life as a piece of furniture. Wood is quite a sensual material, and it is my hope that my work reflects my passion, awe, and respect for these great trees.

"Karnali Lounge Chair." Shown with curly maple frame and black leather upholstery. 29" x 32" x 29". *Courtesy of Michael Traister.*

"Swallowtail Chair." Shown with ebonized walnut frame with cocobolo seat. 26" x 30" x 22". *Courtesy of Michael Traister.*

"Wedge table." Shown in European walnut. Hand-cut corner dovetails and miters. Cherry splines across checks and openings. 60" x 30" x 50". *Courtesy of Michael Traister.*

Charles Ramberg
Charleston, South Carolina

I grew up under the tutelage of my grandfather who taught at St. Paul Vocational School, not as an instructor of woodworking, but as a teacher of radio, TV, and electronics. He was skilled, however, in working with wood. He taught me to believe in myself and my ability to do whatever I put my mind and heart into. He also taught me how to solder wires together before I hit my teen years.

I built my first furniture in high school, a Danish modern couch and two chairs, which were more interesting than the breadboards and birdhouses others chose to build. It took starting another career and becoming disillusioned to finally focus on what I really wanted to do with my life.

Designing and building furniture satisfy my soul. The process of taking an idea, whether from within me or a concept proposed by a client, and making it real, giving it expression in this world we inhabit, is an extraordinary gift. And in honor of that gift, I do everything to preserve the beauty of the wood, the integrity of design and construction, and the durability of the project. So, I see myself partially as an artist, but perhaps more importantly, as a facilitator of people's expression of their needs. Within that context, there is always an awareness of the conscientious use of materials that best suits the divergent project demands.

I love what I do. I enjoy working with people to bring their ideas into reality.

With Honduras mahogany china cabinet. Strip laminated mahogany curved case, 0.25" bent glass, lacquer, and LED lighting. 2006.

"Sport Fish Bar." Teak, mahogany, holly, strip laid planking with fiberglass, high definition glass etching, LED lighting, and lacquer finishes. 84" x 96" x 42" (service height) x 94"(back bar case). 2009.

"Sake Cup Case." Cherry, hard maple, polyester felt, lacquer, and brass. 42" x 39" x 24". 2008.

"Pergola." Spanish cedar, epoxy, custom stainless steel brackets, European technology exterior coating, and cement (piers). 168" x 114" x 64". 2010.

Alfred Sharp

Woodbury, Tennessee

"Elk Side Table." Walnut and glass. 34" x 29" x 20". *Courtesy of John Lucas.*

I'm besotted by wooden furniture from any era, Renaissance to avant-garde. It's been easier to make a living making examples from the seventeenth to nineteenth centuries, so the greater part of my body of work has been in those styles: Jacobean, William and Mary, Queen Anne, Chippendale, Hepplewhite, Sheraton, Federal, French Louis IV - VI, and Biedermeier. Most often, these pieces have not been pure reproductions but rather original designs using period-appropriate elements and motifs. Concurrently, I've made contemporary inspired pieces whenever possible. Even in those instances, however, I tend to look to the past, taking one or more period pieces as a beginning point. Then, by re-writing the rules, altering the proportions, using a more radical wood palette, and generally messing with the expectations that an original piece of furniture might bring to mind, I create my response to the original inspiration.

I'm in awe of my colleagues in the Furniture Society, who seem to be able to pull a truly innovative piece of furniture out of clear air. They really are thinking outside the box. But I remind them often that there are lots of great ideas still inside the box, especially if you shake the box around a little before looking back into it.

I work solely by commission and relish collaborating with my discerning customers to design a piece of furniture that is both fine art and yet entirely functional. Most of my work is done with traditional hand tools, and I qualify as master in carving, marquetry and inlay, advanced construction methods, and French polishing. After nearly forty years, this work continues to be my passion, and I encourage projects that are challenging and difficult.

"Samuel McIntyre Chest-on-Chest." Mahogany. 49" x 108" x 25". *Courtesy of John Lucas.*

"Lady's Writing Desk" (Bonheur du jour). Satinwood 36" x 70" x 19". *Courtesy of John Lucas.*

"Philadelphia Chippendale Arm Chair." Walnut. 27" x 38" x 22".

"Desk." Cherry and sterling silver. 72" x 40" x 30". *Courtesy of John Lucas.*

Courtesy of KC Ramsay

Nick Strange

Carrboro, North Carolina

I've had the good fortune to have a 35-year career in furniture making, the last 29 with my own furniture studio. The English and American Arts and Crafts movements have inspired my passion for furniture making and design. I truly believe the models we use to inspire us greatly influence how we approach our craft. My company is named for another "Century Guild," one founded in 1882 by British architect A. H. Mackmurdo. My goal is to continue the principles followed by those earlier craftsmen and described by Mackmurdo as the willingness "to encourage and establish a high standard of form and method." By constantly challenging my experience with projects that expand my knowledge of design and technique, I continue to learn.

My ecclesiastical work has developed over the years and is a great fit for my philosophy of creating pieces that are legacies for individuals and families for generations to come. It also adds a spiritual element that transcends the usual elements that make my work so satisfying to do. My goal is to design and build pieces that, while unique, also show a command of my craft that is timeless.

"Aumbry." Solid quarter-sawn white oak with water-gilt and polychrome accents. 16" x 47.5" x 9.5". *Courtesy of KC Ramsay.*

"Console." Zebrawood and ebonized pearwood veneers with gaboon ebony solids. 37" x 38" x 22". *Courtesy of KC Ramsay.*

"Telephone Stand." Solid koa with ebony accents and marble top. 30" x 28" x 20". *Courtesy of Richard Faughn.*

"Single-Drawer Desk." Solid mahogany. 48" x 30" x 32.5". *Courtesy of Richard Faughn.*

The South

Doug Turner
Atlanta, Georgia

"Traditional Bookcase." Mahogany and brass. 30" x 40" x 14". *Design/Fabrication: Doug Turner.*

I approach furniture design as a problem solver: I enjoy the challenge of applying the art and science of design to my client's needs. Combining quality, functionality, and beauty in one piece is rarely easy, especially when a limited budget is thrown into the mix. Fortunately, I've worked with some outstanding designers and builders over the years and have learned that all commissioned art is a process and a conversation with a client.

I'm naturally drawn to traditional furniture forms: deep, rich wood tones mixed with aged brass and elegant veneer work. I avoid the heavy ornamentation often found in antique furniture and emphasize the major themes, such as form, color, and pattern. I'm also very inspired by architecture and believe that furniture should complement its environment and become part of the overall design – a design that strives against its surroundings is best reconsidered.

If I had to build one type of furniture for the rest of my life, I'd build bookcases to house my ever-growing art, design, and history library. There's no need to reinvent the wheel; graceful designs work for a reason.

New challenges are a vital aspect of artistic development. I enjoy working on diverse projects, from small occasional tables to massive conference tables, and working with a variety of craftspeople, from stained glass artists to metal fabricators, and learning as much as I can from each of them.

"Traditional Media Cabinet." Mahogany and brass. 72" x 30" x 20". *Design: Doug Turner.*

"Conference Table." Curly ash and walnut. Includes a pop-up TV monitor on the CEO end, and communications, including surface-mounted microphones, and data / electrical plugs. 5'" x 18'" x 30". *Design: Doug Turner/ Coppa Dionne Design.*

"Refectory Table." Ash. 42 "" x 14'" x 30". *Design: Doug Turner. Fabrication: Stephen Evans, Doug Turner.*

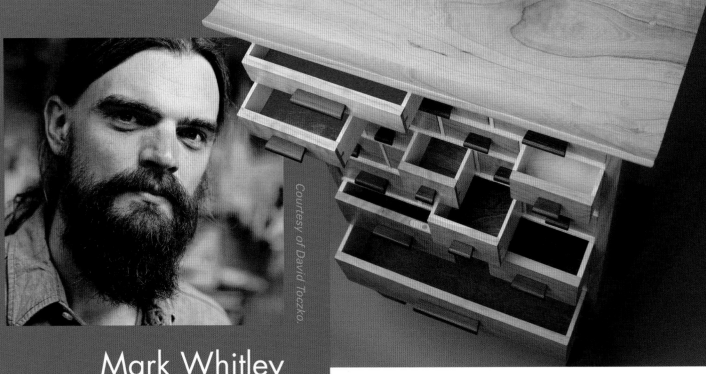

Courtesy of David Toczko.

Mark Whitley

Smiths Grove, Kentucky

"Spectrum: The Necessaries Chest." Cherry, ebonized ash, various dyes, and oil finish. 26" x 48" x 16". 2008. *Courtesy of Wes Davis Photography.*

I approach furniture as functional pieces of art. As a studio craftsman, my primary focus is directed on the holistic aesthetics of the project at hand: the way each piece of wood is joined in harmony with the others. Curves and different species of wood are used in a sparingly and thoughtfully intentional manner so as to enhance the feel of a piece of furniture and keep with the integrity of the design. My work comes from a place deep within that must create objects. I am driven by the satisfaction that comes when the first coat of oil hits the surface and the color and texture of the wood reveal itself before my eyes. Nearly all of my work is built from the walnut, cherry, ash, and maple that grows here in Kentucky and finished with a blend of oils that enhance and protect the wood for generations.

I have been in the shop since I was four years old. In 1999, I began building custom furniture for public sale and commissions. Furniture building for me is not about fast production or pleasing the masses, but about creating pieces that live and breathe in my shop and in your homes. I am as much a craftsman as a person. It is a great gift to spend my life doing what I absolutely love, hopefully enriching the lives of others through the creation of original, well crafted furniture.

Good wood speaks softly
Chips and dust feed my soul's heart
Furniture is born...

"Sculpted Rocker." Cherry, ash, leather, and oil finish. 49" x 49" x 25". 2008. *Courtesy of Wes Davis Photography.*

"Small Wall Cabinet." Cherry, avodire, rosewood, glass, and oil finish. 13" x 28" x 6". 2003. *Courtesy of Wes Davis Photography.*

"Tall Mahogany Cabinet." Mahogany, dyed mahogany, various veneers, glass, and oil finish. 15" x 73" x 14". 2010. *Courtesy of Wes Davis Photography.*

"Barren County Twist." Mahogany, dyed mahogany, various veneers, glass, and oil finish. 54" x 20" x 17". Walnut, mahogany, dyed maple, and oil finish. 2010. *Courtesy of Wes Davis Photography.*

Erik Wolken

Chapel Hill, North Carolina

I like to think of my work as functional sculpture, work that serves a sculptural aesthetic yet does not exist solely to be viewed from afar but to be interacted with and used everyday. There is a rhythm and poetry I seek to create in my pieces, a flow to the lines, a confluence of color and texture that makes a complete statement. My pieces are often the result of a process of discovery. Seldom do I start with a plan written in stone but a series of rough pencil sketches and the belief that I can divine the meaning of a piece in the process of building it.

"Torso No. 4." Wall Hung Cabinet. Carved poplar, paint, maple, and digital imagery. 20" x 34" x 12". 2004.

"Back in the Saddle Again." Coffee table/bench. Laminated ash milk paint and pickled finish. 12" x 51" x 16.5". 2009.

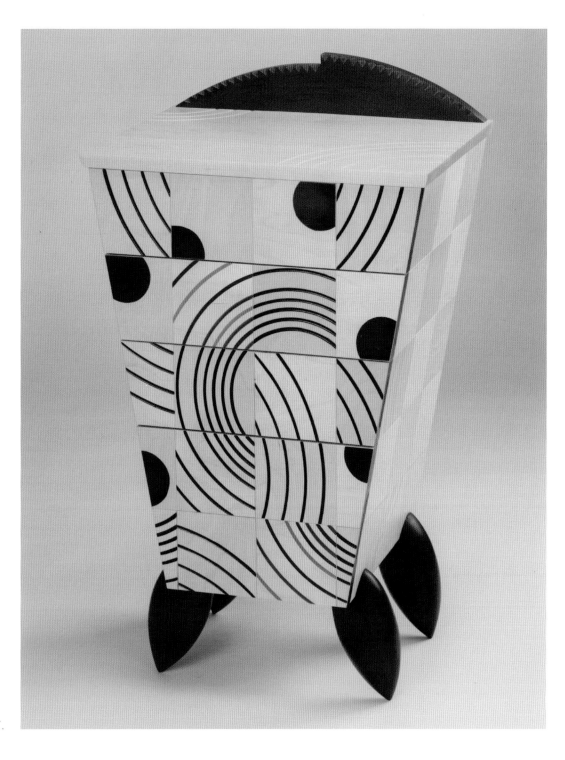

"All Mixed Up." Four-drawer cabinet. Baltic birch plywood, maple, mahogany, and paint. 18" x 28" x 12".

4 The Midwest

Bruce Bartholomew

Bloomington, Indiana

Transforming a rough sawn piece of wood into a beautiful piece of furniture is very gratifying. Knowing that the finished piece is a direct result of my passion and effort is what drew me into furniture making, that and the need for furnishing my own home. As an engineer by trade, details are very important to me, and details are what make the difference between hand built pieces destined to be family heirlooms and mass-produced factory furniture. Family heirlooms should tell a story. When the piece was built is part of that story; for this reason, I inlay a small brass medallion engraved with the year it was built on every piece that I build.

Being self-taught, I always try to incorporate a new aspect to each piece I build. It may be a new technique, tool, or type of wood. Doing this has helped me grow as a furniture maker and stay challenged. The cherry room screen shown is a good example of this approach. I wanted to bring something from my electrical engineering background to the piece. The result was 32 mathematically correct sine-wave dividers created using a bent lamination technique.

If I had to categorize my work, I would say it leans towards classic Shaker style design. I find the uncomplicated lines appealing and functionally elegant. Functionality is key, as I believe a family heirloom should be used, not relegated to a corner and admired from a distance. Furniture should be a part of everyday life, carrying the marks of time left by their owners. Table edges and drawer pulls worn smooth by years of use tell a story of their own.

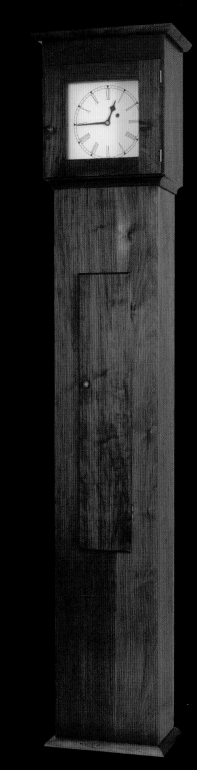

"Shaker Tall Clock." Walnut with varnish finish. 16" x 77" x 10". 2011. *Courtesy of James Kellar.*

"Leaf Keepsake Box." Cherry with mahogany top, walnut handle. 5.5" x 2.5" x 13.75". 2011. *Courtesy of James Kellar.*

"Classic Armoire." Natural cherry with varnish finish. 35" x 26" x 73". 2011. *Courtesy of James Kellar.*

"Sine Wave Room Screen." Cherry with walnut accents. Lacquer finish. 70" x 72" x 0.75". 2011. *Courtesy of James Kellar.*

Reagan Furqueron

Indianapolis, Indiana

My studio practice can be defined by a sense of curiosity, exploration, and an enjoyment for creating objects with my hands. I am trained in traditional furniture making techniques though I am not tied to the tradition of furniture. I rather use those skills to explore ideas through functional and semi-functional forms. These objects manifest themselves through the drawn image, experimentation with material and form, and the execution of works that have implications of physical and visual movement. Physical movement is enacted through the inherent qualities in functional objects, such as the turn of a knob or the opening of drawers and doors. The forms, surface, finish, and color are meant to encourage this, evolving into a play-like relationship.

My new direction of work explores the ideas of growth and transition. I am referencing baskets and nests through representational and abstract forms, combining many elements to define the overall larger entity. Through building, weaving, and the piling of elements, these forms reveal the process of making and visual movement in the textures that create their structure.

"Step Stool." Poplar and milk paint. 15" x 15" x 45". 2004. *Courtesy of Mark Johnston.*

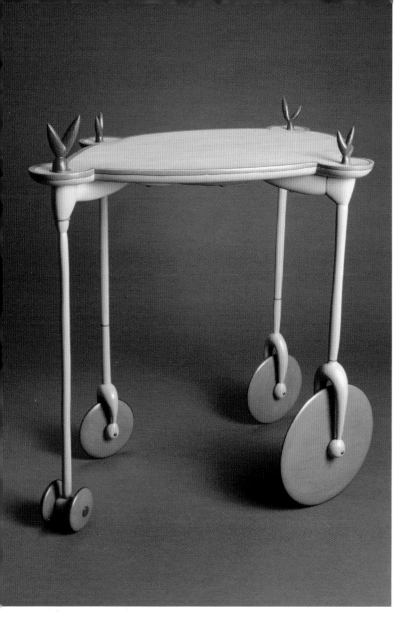

"Rolling Table." Mahogany, metal, and milk paint.
34" x 19" x 35". 2003.

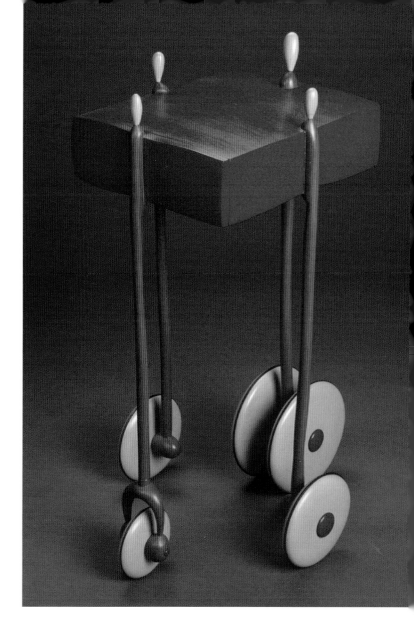

"Rolling Side Table." Mahogany and milk paint,
16" x 13" x 25". 2003.

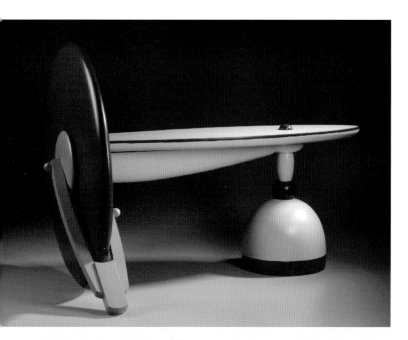

"Coffee Table with Boot." Poplar and milk paint. 40" x 30" x 30.
2010. *Courtesy of Mark Johnston.*

"Nesting Tables." Ash and graphite, 17"" x 17"" x 18". 2009.
Courtesy of Mark Johnston.

Jason Frantz

Springfield, Missouri

Imagine two pieces of furniture, side-by-side, identical in every way: both over a hundred years old, both from the same factory. Your great-grandfather built one. Given the choice, which one would you want? Years ago I came to a startling realization: behind every piece of furniture is a person, someone who dreamt, designed, and created it. Someone who poured their blood, sweat and tears into this one thing. I also realized that I wanted to be that person.

Woodworking is one of those rare undertakings that begins with a material that has beauty and purpose buried deep in its origins. To try to impart more of either can be a daunting task. It can also be intensely rewarding. And while beauty and purpose are vital, the furniture that is most important to us is that which also has meaning.

I think people sometimes forget that furniture does not just spring forth from the forest and gallop into our homes. Craftsmen with sharp tools and keen imaginations create it in a cloud of sawdust and shavings. I can think of no higher honor than to be counted among them.

By the way, if you do know of a forest where furniture skitters around, let me know. I'll start building traps.

With "Martini Bar," home bar in walnut and maple. 2009. *Courtesy of Jensen Images.*

"Bloodwood Butterfly." Elliptical bloodwood table. 30" x 36". 2010. *Courtesy of Jensen Images.*

"Asian Media Center." Lyptus. 26" x 86". 2006. *Courtesy of Edward Biamonte Photography.*

"Ode to a Doorknob." Coat rack. Walnut and maple. 15" x 45". 2011. *Courtesy of Jensen Images.*

"Collapse." Curved birch bookshelf. 18" x 96". 2011. *Courtesy of Jensen Images.*

Tim Gorman

Minneapolis, Minnesota

"Ellipsoid Table." Walnut, oak, maple, bird's eye maple veneer, waterfall bubinga veneer, and ebony. 30" x 46" x 36". 2005. *Courtesy of Petronella Ytsma.*

My furniture invites the viewer to experience it using all the senses. It is warm like skin; it wants you to touch it. Each species of wood has its own distinct smell that can elicit both sensation and memory. A key characteristic of a chair is the creak it makes when you sit in it. In this way, I see my furniture as being characteristically human. It is human in scale because of the way you use it. Joints can be thought of the way a sculptor considers the articulation of a shoulder or elbow. Chairs, tables, and cabinets have arms, legs, backs, shoulders, and knees. Furniture can be sexy, sensuous, charming, demure, muscular, sinuous, masculine, or feminine. These are types of descriptors I seek to embody.

My education and art practice over the last 25 years includes many diverse media and methods, including metalsmithing, jewelry design, industrial design, computer-aided design, drawing, and engineering. Furniture is unique in that it leverages all these interests and skills and challenges me to find new ways of combining them. It demands more of me than any other practice and forces me to refine existing skills while acquiring and developing new ones.

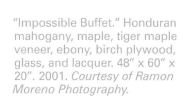

"Impossible Buffet." Honduran mahogany, maple, tiger maple veneer, ebony, birch plywood, glass, and lacquer. 48" x 60" x 20". 2001. *Courtesy of Ramon Moreno Photography.*

"Serpentine Chair." Cherry, ebony, nickel-plated aluminum, stainless steel, and nylon monofilament. 42" x 22" x 30". 2009. *Courtesy of Sarah Whiting.*

"Three Surprises," liquor cabinet. Maple, tiger maple veneer, ebony, neoprene rubber, aluminum, brass, and lacquer. 60" x 24" x 24". 2003. *Courtesy of Ramon Moreno Photography.*

The Midwest

Tom Huang
Lawrence, Kansas

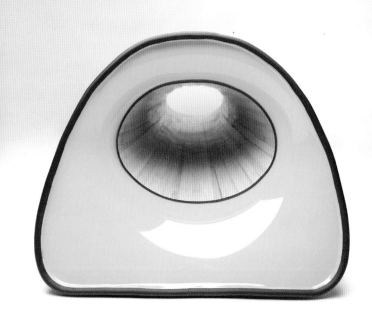

In my work, I look to better understand the global condition of cultural mixing. I enjoy exploring and combining both traditional and non-traditional techniques and materials. As functional objects, in my furniture I hope to suggest the commonality of our basic human utilitarian needs. As sculpture, I celebrate the diversity of various materials and the intrinsic qualities these materials contain. In combining and often weaving bamboo, bronze, rattan, wood, steel, and acrylic, I attempt to bridge gaps between studio furniture, contemporary fiber arts, and sculpture.

I make furniture because these objects address our need to commune. Whether an heirloom vanity, a wall hung mirror, or dining table set for four, these objects enable us to connect with our heritage, our reflected selves, and our loved ones. I believe that each piece I craft is a touchstone of my careful, deliberate, and playful process. My work, in turn, becomes an integral part of my clients' process of developing relationships. My patrons become an integral part of my exploration.

My most recent work uses bamboo flooring planks in techniques developed for canoe and kayak construction. Bamboo's diverse nature and its poetically ubiquitous identity make it the ideal material to carry and express the conceptual basis of my culturally based work.

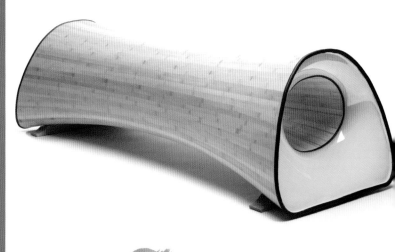

"Infinity." Bench in bamboo, fiberglass, acrylic, and rubber trim. Made in collaboration with Andrew Williams. 60" x 18" x 24". 2011.

"Comfort Girls." Wall-mounted cocktail tables in bamboo, fiberglass, nori, epoxy resin, and glass lenses (built in coasters). 24" x 42" x 16". 2010. *Original retouched by Andrew Williams.*

"WeNotMe." Tea table in mahogany, hand split madake bamboo, and copper wire.
32" x 12.5" x 14". 2009. *Courtesy of Aaron Paden.*

Rick Jasinski

Wyoming, Minnesota

Based in Minnesota, I am a designer and builder of custom, handmade furniture and cabinets crafted from hardwoods. Specializing in many popular styles, from Mission, Arts & Crafts, and Shaker to traditional, contemporary, and modern styles, I transform the furniture vision of my client into a beautiful and enduring one-of-a kind piece.

As a boy, I was introduced to woodworking while watching my uncle build a boat. The selecting and shaping of the wood intrigued me. With a passion instilled at a young age and having been trained as an engineer, I have spent my adult life continually developing my design and furniture building skills. What began as a hobby to design functional furniture pieces for my home has become a long-fulfilled dream to create pieces for the enjoyment of others that are built to the highest level of quality and craftsmanship.

I believe a fine piece of furniture is born when a craftsman who understands its character shapes a distinctive piece of wood. I have always loved the beauty of wood: its unique shapes, colors, and grains. I strive to display that beauty in my designs. I am inspired by the craftsmanship of older furniture styles, particularly Shaker and Arts & Crafts, which are characterized by simple utilitarian design and mastery of the dovetail and mortise and tenon joinery. I strive to combine the wood's' character and exposed joinery with the functional requirements of modern furniture in each of my pieces.

"Combination Gun and Bow Cabinet."
Red oak hardwood with etched glass panes.

"Book or DVD Case." Red oak hardwood with antique glass door inserts.

"Shaker Baby Crib" and "Changing Table."
The laminated spindles of maple hardwood are attached with mortise and tenon joinery.

"Country French Armoire." Maple hardwood featuring arched panel doors and flush mount drawers.

Christine Chovan Studio C3.

George Mahoney
Minneapolis, Minnesota

My work as a furniture designer is in a constant state of growth. Architecture, fashion, graphic, and object design are major inspirations for me. These have helped guide my practice as I explore the artistic disciplines of the minimal, modern, and organic. The intermingling of these influences result in an original and powerful language that speaks through my furniture both physically and visually.

Using new and different material in my furniture reinforces the physical and visual presence of each individual piece. The relationship established between varying materials creates cohesiveness within the design and affects an object's function and overall aesthetic. The material-driven nature assists in establishing the design and can even help direct it. The intuitive action in the studio is also critical, ensuring that the end result is an authentic object.

"Evans." Ebonized bent birch plywood, water-based polyurethane, and stainless steel frame.
25" x 35" x 29.5". 2007.

"Metropolis." Formed fiberglass and Kevlar hoops, giant fabric, high dense foam, powder-coated mild-steel frame, and stainless steel hardware.
28" x 32" x 32". 2005.

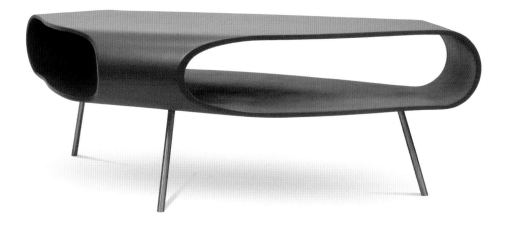

"Molecule Gray" and "Molecule Group." Bentwood, paint, clear-coat, and stainless steel. 42" x 26" x 18". 2011.

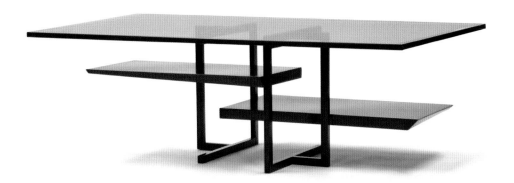

"LJC Flat," cocktail table. Cold-rolled steel frame, hollowed formed steel shelves, black patina, wax, and glass. 32" x 52" x 17". 2007.

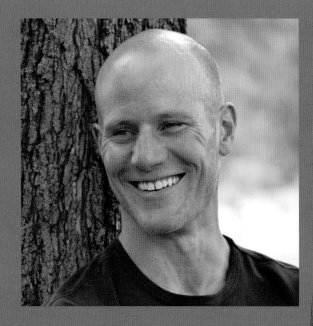

David Michael Redwine

Brooklyn, Wisconsin

"Jewelry Armoire." Swiss pearwood and Honduras rosewood. 14" x 7" x 5". 2006.

People who learn that I am a furniture designer and maker often ask me how or when I became interested in it. What I think they're really after is the why. If they have a little extra time on their hands, I tell them the story about how, at the tender age of 7, I found an old birdhouse tucked away in my parents' garage. This birdhouse was weathered grey from past use, but not in bad shape. I decided then and there that what it needed in order to be useful again was a post, a couple of nails, and a place to be. That place would be in our own front yard. The nails would come from the rusty can in the basement. And the post? The post would present itself, almost mystically, in our neighbor's front yard. Once I'd located a saw, it wasn't long before their young maple sapling had a new home and purpose in the snow bank next to our driveway. Of course, as the spring sun came on in earnest, gravity began to exert itself on my failing project. (I like to think of it as my first prototype.) Predictably, the neighbors' suspicions were cast in my direction. The jig, as they say, was up.

Because trees, birds, water, and wind have always surrounded and shaped the lens through which I view things, these elements necessarily provide the form for my design. Nowadays, I relish designing and making functional art for the same reason I did as a child – namely, because there is a need for it. When I meet that need with skill, passion, and patience, I am being who I am and who I want to be. I am being an artist.

"Wave Coffee Table." American black walnut. 42" x 42" x 18". 2011.

"Wish Table." Hickory. 72"-112" x 42" x 30". 2008. *Nicole Cooke Photography.*

"Spirit Chair." Bleached hard maple and leather. 36" x 22" x 18". 2007. *Nicole Cooke Photography.*

The Midwest

Sylvie Rosenthal

Madison, Wisconsin

"The Chase," mirror. Poplar, plywood, cherry, steel, silver, and paint. 26" x 48" x 5". 2006.
Courtesy of Steve Mann.

Serendipity put tools in my hands, and I trained to be an artisan. My furniture refused to stay furniture. It spoke in ironic quips. It asked questions. It made statements.

My work has always dealt with transformation. From the inside out, how to get there from here? Content driven, a bit personal, and steeped in the impossible. From snakes swallowing teapots to kinetic birds acting as guides, stacking chests to store your hopes to a kinetic boat drifting on a waterless sea. It speaks to how we must always change, evolve, fall, hope, hurt, love, recover, remember, and forget. It is our evolutionary heritage to look for balance in the imbalance and uncertainty.

Currently, my work fits in a more transient space, one in between imagined and reality. I crave the uncertainty of improbable imagery. The newest work combines carved animal forms, vernacular architecture, and furniture objects. I am working with shifts in scale, impossible places that are believable, and how through these changes we look at our built and natural worlds. The juxtapositions are a way to find the space between objects, life, and the built environment. Architectural and furniture references invite viewers to imagine themselves within these spaces. Small chairs, stools, and tables are placeholders. You know what to do with them, imagine yourself inside, and the work becomes monumental or you become miniature. How does that feel? Stacking and piling small furniture is controlled chaos. The piles become things, like an elephant, domestic objects gone feral.

It is a practice of expanding and blending, where is the crossover? What is the crossover? I am interested in un-domesticating to create a new space. Why does this whale have a roof rack? We fill in the blanks.

"Birdie Suite." Mahogany, poplar, white oak, milk paint, steel, plywood, and mixed media. Desk: 34" x 69" x 20". chair: 17" x 19.5" x 15". 2007. *Courtesy of Steve Mann.*

"Hope by Hope." Poplar, mahogany, plywood, acrylic paint, and mixed media. 40" x 63" x 22.5". 2009. *Courtesy of Steve Mann.*

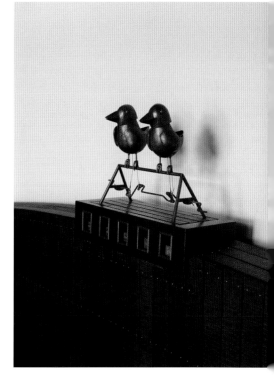

"Beau's Bed." Poplar, pine, mahogany, black gesso, steel, and mixed media. Head board 83" x 54" x 5". Foot board 83" x 24" x 4". 2009. *Courtesy of Judy Sirota Rosenthal.*

Larion Swartzendruber

Goshen, Indiana

"Pub Collection." Quarter sawn curly maple. *Photo – Echols' Photographics.*

I remember loving woodworking as a small child. I then studied to be an Industrial Arts Teacher and taught high school students for five years. Furniture making went from a hobby to a passion, and I started my furniture business near the end of my first year of teaching. Over the years I have found that "well" designed and built furniture can only be termed excellent if all of the elements are superbly executed.

The designs need to be well proportioned, need to function well for their intended use and stay true to the "period" of choice, and blend well with their surroundings.

The wood selection is very important. Beautiful wood adds so much to the piece if it has the proper grain character, is nicely matched for color, and has pleasing grain patterns.

The pieces have to be cut with precision for good joinery and perfect surface quality.

Great sanding and finishing will give the surfaces a nice "silky smooth feel" and will show beautiful natural looking grain and make pleasing transparent stains and finish coats possible.

I sincerely believe there is a distinct difference in the furniture built by craftsmen who are artists, deriving great satisfaction from what they do!

"Prairie Settle with Table Arms." Quarter sawn white oak. *Photo – Echols' Photographics.*

"Contemporary Entertainment Center." Cherry and carpathian elm. *Photo – Echols' Photographics.*

"French Country Armoire." Cherry.
Photo – Echols' Photographics.

"Torus Table" with leaves and leaf rack. Cherry. *Photo – Echols' Photographics.*

The Midwest

Edward Wohl

Ridgeway, Wisconsin

With figured walnut settee. 2007. *Courtesy of Al Lada.*

I make things of wood that I'd like to have myself: functional pieces that are quiet, peaceful, and a pleasure to touch and look at. My approach emphasizes select materials, structural integrity, and utility. I like to let the wood do the work, to coax nature to imitate art.

For more than forty years, I have been designing and building furniture and growing a company that sells bird's eye maple cutting boards worldwide. I think of myself as a designer-craftsman rather than a studio artist. My primary source of learning, encouragement, and inspiration comes from my decades-long friendship and working relationship with industrial designer Bill Stumpf. Projects built with or for Bill emphasized function, masterful design, seamless joinery, and liquid smooth finishes – lessons I have applied to everything I have ever built. I always think in terms of multiples rather than one-off pieces. I am happiest when I am in the shop, working with the tools of the trade.

A mission statement, sort of

I disguise trees.
Fellers trundle them in
slabs, and stack them
crosswise in a darkened waiting room.

I fret and pace: which are the ready
candidates? What shape and function
will console the Cherry, cut forever from
its fruitful reign?

What would the Burr Oak now become,
having been protector and provider for grey
squirrels of distinguished lineage
for (count the rings) so many generations?

Maybe this—no, rather, that—I grieve
Until you call and say you need
a place to sit, to store your Sunday suits
or hold your pots and pans or treasures.

You free my mind so hand and eye can
go to work. The wood and I conspire;
we have to please all three of us. Success
means we all live a little longer.

"Jewelry Box." Bird's eye maple. 22" x 12" x 16". 2002. *Courtesy of Al Lada.*

"Desk." Figured cherry. 80" x 29" x 36". 2010. *Courtesy of Al Lada.*

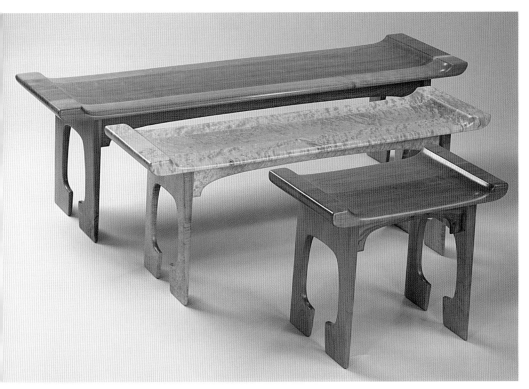

"Benches." 2005. *Courtesy of Al Lada.*

"Dining Table." Bird's eye maple. 9'" x 4'" x 29" high. "Dining Chairs." Cherry. 2005. *Courtesy of Eric Ferguson.*

5 | The West

David Delthony

Escalante, Utah

With "Offering," an occasional table in laminated/sculpted plywood.

For over 30 years, my life has been thoroughly intertwined with the "Sculptured Furniture" that I create. The realization of this endeavor has taken me from New York to West Berlin, Germany, where I earned my Master Cabinet Makers Certification and a degree in interior design at the Academy of Fine Arts. Fifteen years ago, I relocated to the canyon and slick rock country of southern Utah, where my organic, sculptured forms find their counterpart in the beauty of the natural surroundings.

The focus of my work has always been the dialogue between functional and aesthetic values, and I have tried to balance these in each object. As a studio furniture artist, my designs are sculpted in wood, utilizing the inherent qualities of the material and my knowledge of ergonomics to create comfortable, functional organic forms. Working within the concept and syntax of fine furniture, I infuse my work with an artistic sensuality, embracing visual and tactile senses and encouraging the human contact that defines my vision as an artist.

All of my pieces are created through the process of laminating woods, which allows me to create stronger and more complex designs. Currently, I use solid plywood in pieces such as the "Sculptured Chair III" and the rocking chair "Lotus," since the material is suitable for creating intricate and sometimes cantilevered constructions. It has always been my intent to combine the artistic image (sculpture), function (ergonomics), and fine craftsmanship into the organic, flowing forms of my work. I feel strongly that artistic creation should be incorporated into our daily surroundings and attempt to realize this through my own visual language. Because of the complex nature of the process, my work is limited to less than 10 pieces per year.

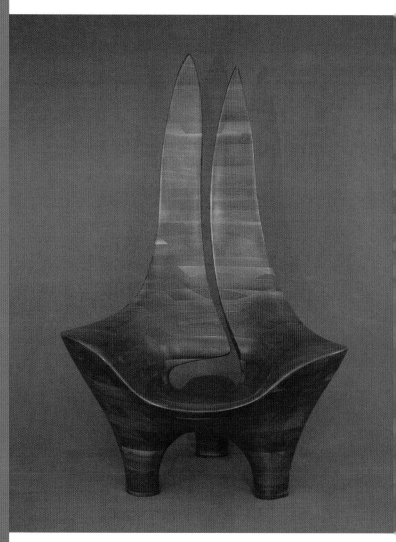

"King's Chair IV." Laminated/sculpted black walnut. 41" x 29" x 62". 2008.

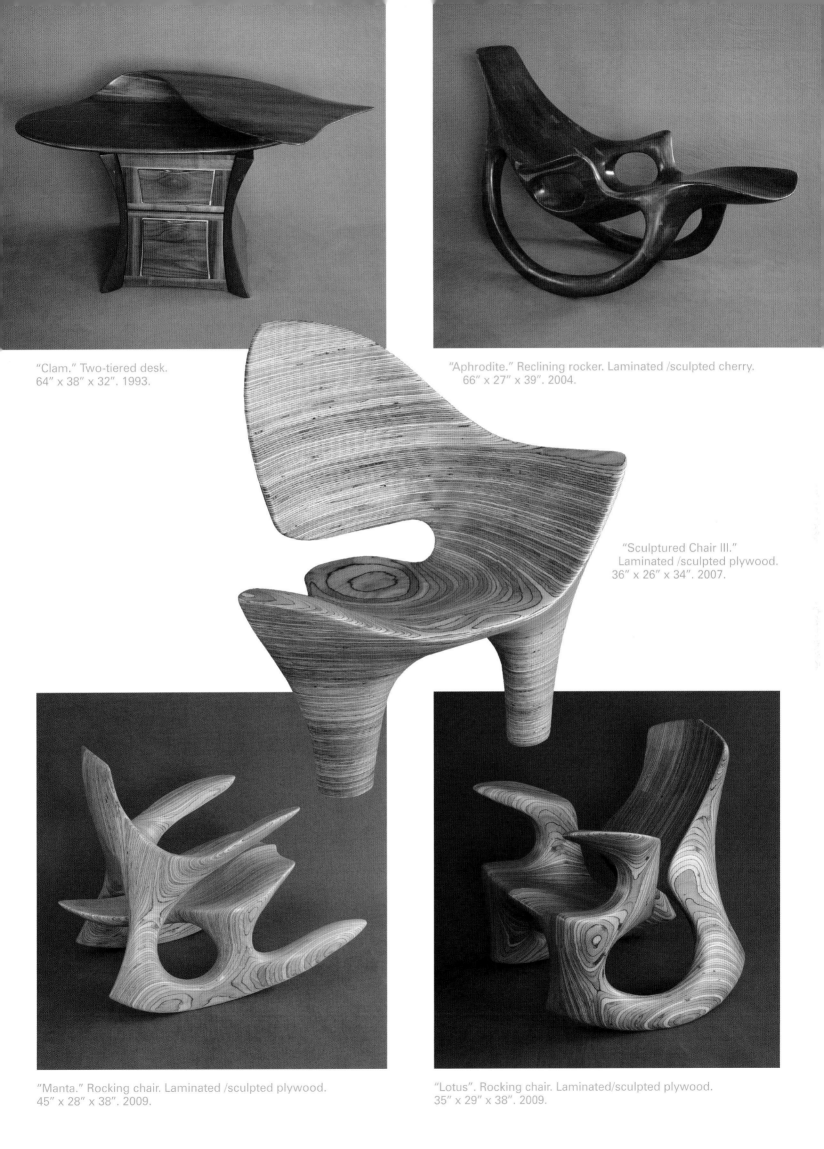

"Clam." Two-tiered desk.
64" x 38" x 32". 1993.

"Aphrodite." Reclining rocker. Laminated /sculpted cherry.
66" x 27" x 39". 2004.

"Sculptured Chair III."
Laminated /sculpted plywood.
36" x 26" x 34". 2007.

"Manta." Rocking chair. Laminated /sculpted plywood.
45" x 28" x 38". 2009.

"Lotus". Rocking chair. Laminated/sculpted plywood.
35" x 29" x 38". 2009.

The West

Courtesy of Jacqueline Beam.

Scott Ernst
Glorieta, New Mexico

"Goodman Media Cabinet." Walnut and walnut burl. 65" x 42" x 20". 2006. *Courtesy of Fred Knight Photography.*

Building furniture is fun and difficult. Or, more to the point, building furniture is fun because it is difficult. I love that, no matter how many years I work with wood and build furniture, there will be more to learn, more unique pieces to design, more styles to be inspired by, and more technical challenges to overcome. For me, the beauty of working in a craft is that it combines the need for the eye of an artist with the mind of an engineer. You design a piece of furniture that is well proportioned, functional, and aesthetically pleasing; then you have to work backward to figure out how it should be constructed. Often the design will force you to work the material in some completely new way, to think outside of any of the boxes you may have been working from in the past. It is aesthetic and technical. It is chin-scratching, creative problem solving every day.

Much of my work is designed with a specific client in mind. I see it as portraiture in wood, and I take into account my client's tastes, personality, and functional needs when I'm working on a design. At times, there is a give and take – a call and response – with the client that is not unlike two jazz musicians improvising on a tune. We start with a theme and toss ideas back and forth: each one inspiring and being inspired by the ideas of the other until we have come up with something that is more than either of us. When it really works, it is magic. It is alchemy: the forming of something beautiful and lasting, where, before, there was just a lump of wood.

"Lines Bedside Cabinet." White oak. 36" x 16" x 32". 2007. *Courtesy of Fred Knight Photography.*

"Lanier Kitchen Island." Big leaf maple burl, acrylic, steels. 36" x 36" x 42". 2006. *Ben Tremper Photography.*

"Diamond Sideboard." Zebrawood. 66" x 19" x 36". 2006. *Courtesy of Fred Knight Photography.*

"Oei Make-Up Table". French walnut. 72" x 20" x 30". 2005. *Courtesy of Fred Knight Photography.*

Courtesy of David Cook

Derek Hurd

Boise, Idaho

I moved west as a young man, from the green hills of Vermont to the rugged mountains of Montana, in pursuit of a professional degree in architecture. After acquiring my masters of architecture at Montana State, my wife Danielle and I migrated south, out of the snow, to amazing Boise, Idaho. Since then, I have been designing custom homes nationwide and am a founding partner of Gravitas, Inc., an award-winning residential design firm. I split my time and have found a peaceful balance in my life with the macro design of the whole home joined with the hands-on micro design and fabrication of furniture.

Recent projects have focused on the marriage between wood and steel. They emphasize the natural beauty of the wood and highlight the inorganic qualities of the steel. Through simplification, distraction is removed, allowing the wood and steel to have a pleasant, quiet conversation. I have also been enjoying projects that integrate and incorporate reclaimed and repurposed materials and objects. On these pages, you can see examples of that with old doors and vintage vacuums. There are so many objects around us every day that can be given new life in a one-of-a-kind piece of furniture.

You will also notice some urns as examples of my work. The urns are included because they have deep meaning to me as I make them and to the families that purchase them. There is a unique spirit in the studio when I make urns; it's quiet, it's pensive, and it's contemplative, a welcome pace in this world.

"Gravitas Conference Table." Re-laminated Microllam, and steel. 72" x 36" x 32". 2001. Design and creation in collaboration with Gravitas, Inc.

"Modern Urns." Black limba, walnut, and zinc. 8" x 5" x 6". 2010.

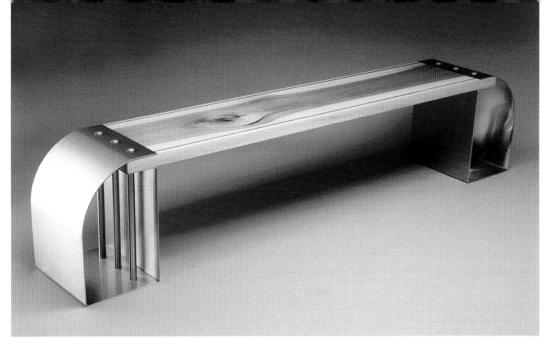

"Boise Contemporary Theater Benches." Stainless steel, poplar slab, and walnut. 80" x 14" x 18". 2004. *Courtesy of Bob Pluckebaum.*

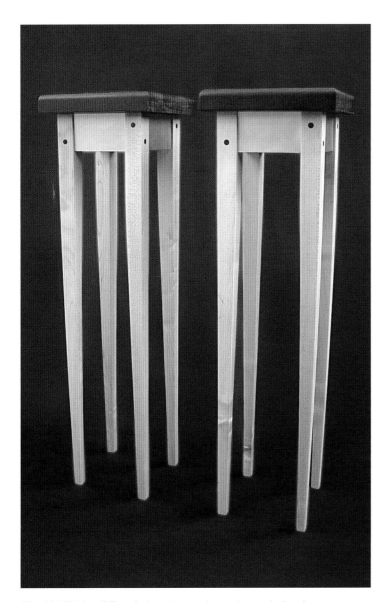

"Orchid Tables." Purple heart, mard maple, and aluminum. 9" x 9" x 32". 2005.

"Atomic Tables." Repurposed 1954 Electrolux, glass, and stainless steel. 18" x 18" x 24". 2008.

Courtesy of Jennifer Fischer.

Harv Mastalir

Black Hawk, Colorado

I have been producing award-winning custom furniture and accessories since 1981. My work has been shown nationally in galleries and museums and resides in homes all across the country. I work alone and, as each piece is custom designed, I work on only one piece at a time. As a self-taught woodworker, I believe one of the responsibilities of a craftsperson is to pass on knowledge to aspiring woodworkers. To this end, I have been teaching classes and workshops in schools, art centers, and my studio since 1989.

I believe furniture is first and foremost functional; it is to be used. It should fit the contours of our lives as well as our bodies. To this end, I apply traditional, and frequently ancient construction techniques to contemporary one-of-a-kind designs. My designs are modest. I strive for clean, elegant lines and simplicity, incorporating quiet details and accents to enhance visual vitality.

I like the way wood looks, feels, and smells. It's a responsive material; it can be worked with crude stone implements or finely tuned precision tools. I prefer using North American native species rather than imported exotics. Domestic woods are quite beautiful and using them does not contribute to the destruction of the tropical rain forests.

For me, woodworking is a continuous exploration of material, form and function. My work reflects this personal inquiry into wood, technique, and design.

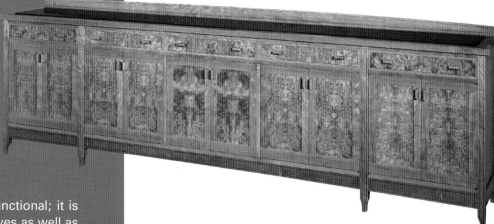

"Sideboard." Cherry, maple burl, costello, and granite. *Courtesy of Russell McDougal/Photo Imaging.*

"Eight-Drawer Dresser." Cherry and bird's eye maple. *Courtesy of Russell McDougal/Photo Imaging.*

"Woven Top Hall Table." Cherry, curly ash, and ebony. *Courtesy of Russell McDougal/Photo Imaging.*

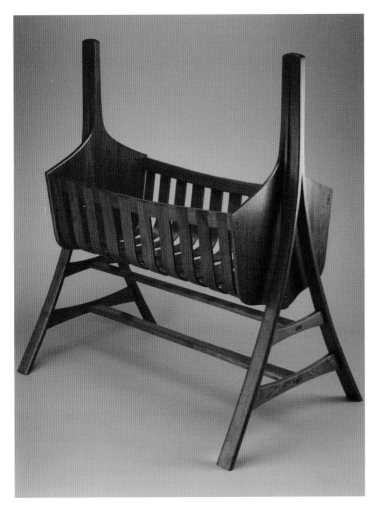

"Cradle." Walnut. *Courtesy of Tim Benko/Benko Photography.*

"Dining Table with Leaves." Walnut and maple. *Courtesy of Tim Murphy/Foto Imagery.*

The West

Courtesy of David Clifford Photography.

David Rasmussen

Carbondale, Colorado

I am a maker. I have been making objects of art and utility since I was young. I find great pleasure and satisfaction sharing my creations with those who will cherish and enjoy them. I find it necessary in a world where short-term thought is so prevalent to create object that will outlast their patrons. Every piece of furniture I create is intended to become an heirloom of a future generation.

I use traditional joinery techniques in my work to ensure that that the pieces I create are heirloom quality. I work with wood, metal, cardboard, eco resin, plastic, cork, and many other materials in my work. No two pieces are exactly alike. The mark of the hand is important in my work. I make sure the every piece expresses its handmade nature.

In terms of design, my work is a response to what I see as modern culture. I see inspiration in pop art, architecture, nature, and in modern design. My furniture is a vision of what I think to be relevant and thought provoking within the realm of modern culture. In my work, I use simple clean forms with elements of contrast.

"Artichoke Table." The Artichoke table was designed to represent an organic form that has been split to reveal its core, in this case the cross section of an artichoke. The body of the table is made from shop-molded plywood faced with exceptional zebrawood veneer and coopered to form the elliptical shell. Cocobolo legs are mortised into the shell to make this table heirloom quality. Artist Scott Harris skillfully executed the acrylic painting on the top of the table. The painting has been sanded flat and treated to act as a durable tabletop. 20" x 21.75". 2010. *Courtesy of David Rasmussen Design.*

"Modern Console." Spalted maple, wenge, and stainless steel. 72" x 24" x 18". 2011. *Courtesy of David Rasmussen Design.*

"Branching Table." The base is custom-forged steel with a black patina. The top is a single piece of exceptionally figured claro walnut. 38" x 42". 2010.

"Overlap Table." The top of this table is made from a single slab of cherry. Two squares of bubinga overlap the cherry slab to support the top and give emphasis to the organic shape. A rosewood butterfly key is inlayed into the slab to give structure to a check that formed as the slab was cured. 24" x 64" x 18". 2009. *Courtesy of David Rasmussen Design.*

"Tree Core Bed." The head and footboard are the cross sections of the log. The curving tree rings on the head and footboard are made of thin strips of bubinga inlayed into Douglas fir veneer. 94" x 54" x 90". 2009. *Courtesy of David Rasmussen Design.*

The West

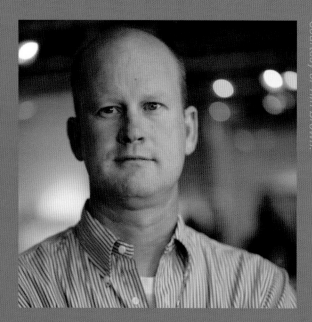

Courtesy of Tim Brown.

Kent Townsend

Salida, Colorado

Creating one-of-a-kind furniture represents a unique blending of the beauty, elegance, and materials of the natural world and the creative spirit of one's imagination. I studied furniture making at the College of the Redwoods in northern California, a program renowned for its excellence in craftsmanship and attention to detail. There, I developed an extensive background in traditional cabinetmaking techniques and hand skills. The focused environment became the setting for me to explore complex forms and develop as an artist. I continued my education at Capellagarden (Sweden), a school with a long history in design and detailed craftsmanship. There, I further developed my sense of materials, form, and composition.

My inspiration comes from nature, Asian arts, and the work of some of the great designers/makers of the past, e.g., Jacques-Emile Ruhlman and Edward Barnsley. My current work is influenced by the Art Deco style: I enjoy its refined form and technical nature.

I enjoy the challenge of complex design, the uncertainty that goes along with this type of work, and how completely involved I have to be. My goal is to create works that are enduring, aesthetically pleasing, and made to the highest level of my ability.

"Coffee Table." Zircote. 42" x 16" x 42". 2010.
Courtesy of Tim Brown.

"Desk." Macassar ebony and Swiss pear.
55" x 30" x 26". 2003. *Courtesy of Tim Brown.*

"Bubinga Cabinet." Bubinga, silver, and ebony.
50" x 36" x 18". 2011. *Courtesy of Tim Brown.*

"Credenza." Macassar ebony. 66" x 36" x 18". *Courtesy of Tim Brown.*

The West

Courtesy of Nyna Cunningham Dolby.

Rex D. White

Fredericksburg, Texas

My mission is to design and craft beautiful furniture that will fit my clients' needs and add something to their surroundings and their lives. Creating heritage pieces that families will enjoy for generations is one of my goals. For example, I aim to design and build a dining room suite, where families gather and warm memories are created. Or, craft my own "Ribbonback Rocker" that will get passed from mother to daughter to granddaughter. Or, construct the days-gone-by hope chest that holds treasures for the future.

As a woodworker, designer, and craftsman, I create individual pieces of furniture that are of superior quality and design. All pieces are hand-finished to a silky smoothness that brings out the natural beauty of the finest hardwoods. Different projects call for different types of wood. I choose each piece of wood for its natural color and grain, and then show that off. I provide the same attention to detail to the bottom, back, and inside of a piece as I do to the easily viewed/touched surfaces.

Based upon my background (BS civil engineering) and training (AOS in woodworking and furniture design from the Wendell Castle Workshop, Scottsville, NY), I focus on the functionality of my pieces and the construction techniques to build them. My pieces are based upon traditional or contemporary designs and are adjusted to meet each client's individual style. Be it a desk, a bed, a table, or a fireplace mantel, the client comes to me to fill a need. When I discover what someone wants or needs, I then bring all that together in a beautiful, functional, finished product that will be a delight to experience.

"Pencil Post Bed," queen size. Walnut. 2005. *Courtesy of White Oak Studio.*

Chest of Drawers. Curly maple and wenge. 66" x 39.5" x 21". 2005. *Courtesy of White Oak Studio.*

"Ribbon Back Chair." Walnut and leather. 20" x 40" x 19.5". 1999. *Courtesy of White Oak Studio.*

"Ribbon Back Rocker." Cherry. 29" x 44". 2000. *Courtesy of White Oak Studio.*

"Campaign Desk." Wenge and cherry. 72" x 30" x 36". 2006. *Courtesy of White Oak Studio.*

"Stand-up Desk." Curly cherry, curly koa, and lacewood. 37" x 57" x 29.25". 2009. *Courtesy of White Oak Studio.*

6 The Far West

Tom Calhoun
Makawao, Hawaii

With "Birds in the Rain" carved panel. Honduras mahogany. 12.75" x 18.5". 2009.

I love story telling. Visual arts are the expressions of our shared human drama through the joining of excellent handcraft and sensitive story craft. Whether I am telling a story from the native Hawaiian culture of my home, from one of the many cultures that now inhabit Hawaii, from a client's life experience, or my own personal story, it is the work of finding a focused visual presentation that defines the shapes and materials of a piece.

The magic of highly figured Koa, the broader palette of the many trees – native or not – now growing here, and all the other woods imported from all over the world help to make Hawaii a joy for the art of woodworking. The sun and wind through verdant slopes, the constant movement of stream and sea, the ever-changing open skies all provide unrivalled inspiration.

Such inspiration needs to be accompanied by an even greater amount of perspiration (to paraphrase Thomas Edison). Woodworking in the long view is not only shop work; it is also planting more trees than I will ever hope to use. The work of felling, milling, stacking, and drying are also parts of the process often better not left to others as their focus may not be the quality and final use of the wood.

My art constantly challenges me physically, mentally, aesthetically, and emotionally. What started as a creative endeavor has grown into a lifestyle I cannot imagine not living.

"GEM." Curly koa veneers. 2004.
Photo by Hal Lum.

"Kaiea Elua." Figured koa, Italian cypress, and Brazilian quartzite. 48" x 34" x 43". 2002.
Photo by Xinia Productions.

"Torii." Figured koa, bamboo, and spalted tamarind. 11" x 42" x 30". 2006.

"Ulu'ohe." Figured Koa, koa veneers, satinwood veneers, mango wood, and marble 10" x 42" x 10" x 30". 2002. *Photo by Xinia Productions.*

"Waterfalls." I was aiming at an Art Deco look with the movement of Art Nouveau. The base is veneered in black dyed Koto, the water is Japanese Tamo Ash veneers, and the "background" is some large, heavily quilted Makore veneer. 17" h. x 25" w. x 51" l. 2009.

Stephen Courtney

Los Angeles, California

"Modern Side Table." Ash wood veneer against bent plywood form; spun metal, perforated stainless steel bowl and rim; birdshot beneath sandblasted glass top; stain finish. 25" x 25". 2001. *Courtesy of Ken Merfeld.*

A freehand sketch. A profile. Often, notes on a café napkin. Such a simple start. But it's enough. The design, the lines are there. From there: hand-generated drawings, elevations, sections, and dimensions. Nothing sophisticated. And not always to scale. But again, enough to run with.

Thereafter, full-scale layouts; cardboard or thin plywood mock-ups. This is where the inner and outer eye meet and wrestle. Here, the keen eye studies proportions, dimensions, and details. Typically, it's a matter of subtraction. An adjustment to a radius, the taper to a leg. Reduce, refine. A return to the original design sketch that sparked the journey.

When ready, the full-scale templates are created, wood species selected – and the millwork begins. Tools in hand help harness an active mind. Creating jigs; seeking solutions to realize difficult design elements; shaping legs; making forms for curved parts; clamping/gluing up: the entire creative process brings great satisfaction.

Primarily a woodworker, I welcome the mix of materials, earth elements such as wood, metal, stones, and hides. I also like color and a hint of humor. Humor – it brings a smile and surrounds a piece with a sense of spirit. Humor softens, lightens, and invites easy interaction. I try to build this element into most pieces – where sensible, and where it can integrate, elevate a piece without a notion of gimmick. It is nothing to be forced. It's a natural when it works.

Modern, dynamic, and different. That's the furniture in design I respond to most. I prize innovation, originality. I love furniture: I know the vocabulary; I speak the language. I appreciate the borders, the boundaries, defined by furniture's fundamental purpose: to serve the human form and to enrich the human experience.

Near the bone, it's sculpture. But it's not. It's furniture. That's just the starting point… where our common language begins. When thinking "studio/bespoke" furniture, I take shelter beneath the term "functional art." I invite and encourage contact.

"Golf-Tee Secretarial Desk." Maple wood; thousands of golf-tees beneath bent glass hood; drop-down desk top; stainless steel elements; stain finish. Original acquired by the National Museum of Art, Smithsonian Institution. 43" x 48" x 24". 1998. *Courtesy of Vu Ong.*

"Century Coffee Table." Walnut veneer against plywood form, fabricated steel base, steel form outline elements, long-hair-on-cow with giraffe pattern beneath glass top. 53" x 16" x 30". 2000. *Courtesy of Ken Merfeld.*

The Far West

With an etched glass walnut hutch.

Don DeDobbeleer

Etna, California

"Serpentine Curved Front Cabinet." Bolivian rosewood, macassar ebony, bloodwood, and wenge. 53" x 44" x 28". *Courtesy of Stanley Krute/skcaps.com.*

I have been making furniture since my high school days in wood shop. I was fortunate to have an instructor who stressed geometry instead of math. This approach has helped me throughout my career as a furniture designer and builder. Understanding and executing proper proportions are critical in my designs. I am driven to build furniture; it's not an option for me. I have never had much interest in producing period pieces but borrow design elements from across the spectrum for my designs. Often the Asian influence creeps in without my realizing it, until the final sketches are evaluated. Sometimes, the client's ideas for a particular piece will take me into uncharted waters. Trying to blend dissimilar pieces of furniture, in a client's home, with a unifying new piece, can be a daunting design task. The blending of different design elements into a cohesive piece is an enjoyable challenge for me. The excitement begins from the moment I select the wood and continues all through the construction process, culminating in the intense feelings of accomplishment, as I apply that first coat of finish. Only then, can I see the colors and textures that have been hidden in the raw wood. Small elements seem to come to life, and painstaking details suddenly seem to come to the forefront. Then I realize, once again, there are no small details. Every piece is a part of the whole, and I just know when it all works, and the design blends all those elements into a cohesive piece of furniture that is music to the eye.

"The Dogwood Chest." Cherry, claro walnut, holly, canary wood, and alder. 40" x 22" x 18". *Courtesy of Stanley Krute/skcaps.com.*

"Demilune Table." Claro walnut, redwood lace burl, wenge, and maple. 38" x 28" x 13". *Courtesy of Stanley Krute/skcaps.com.*

"Dining Table and Chairs." Bolivian rosewood and maple. 50" x 30" x 82" (extending to 122"). *Courtesy of Stanley Krute/skcaps.com.*

Mats Fogelvik
Ocean View, Hawaii

I am a custom woodworker, consistently reaching for the highest standards of quality. I have been building most of my life, from houses, to cabinetry and finally furniture. In 1992, I moved from Sweden to Hawaii; it wasn't really planned, just one of those adventures that happens in life's destiny. Getting married also sealed the deal. I enjoyed being on the islands, and the beautiful local woods, especially Acacia Koa, amazed me. In 1996, I started my furniture making business, Fogelvik Furniture, and I have been working with the local woods, making custom woodwork and furniture. Koa wood is unusual because it varies a lot in color and grain; some of it can be very figured and curly, and in certain light it has an almost holographic effect in the way it refracts multiple hues. I have made it my priority to create original designs, using mostly this special wood. I like to go for the "Wow" effect, creating pieces that evoke responses from the viewer. I do a lot of work with veneers as well, which allows me more design freedom than solid wood. It also gives me more yield from the expensive high-grade koa wood.

"Kapa Poho." Cabinet on stand, East Indian walnut, primavera, mango, koa and various hardwood veneers. 60" tall. 2011. *Courtesy of Hal Lum.*

"The Jewel." Sideboard/cabinet. Curly koa with details of wenge and holly. 60" x 32". 2007.

"Nihoniho." Demi-lune table. Curly koa. 32" tall. 2010.

"Wailuaiki Side Table." Koa, imbuya, olive ash burl, and rosewood. 60" x 32". 2009.

"Lava Fountain." Sofa table. Curly koa with holly inlay. 48" square. 2010. *Courtesy of Hal Lum.*

Roger Heitzman

—— Scotts Valley, California

For many years I have been fascinated by functional art. For me the most appealing approach has been through furniture and its most natural medium, wood. I have always felt that furniture should do more than simply serve a practical purpose; I feel it should also offer a unique visual expression that enhances and transcends function. Ideally, this expression will come from a skillful blend of distinct visual design and high quality craftsmanship.

There is a specific challenge within each new piece in that there should always be a unique harmony between visual design, function, and construction. It is always an exciting moment when that harmony is found, whether on the drawing board or on the workbench. For me, there are few occupations that offer such a tangible and lasting reward.

In addition to designing and creating custom furniture, I have been a woodworking techniques instructor at Marc Adams School of Woodworking in Franklin, Indiana (2002 and 2004) and an instructor of Furniture Design at Foothill DeAnza College in Cupertino, California (1996-1998).

"Deco Hall Table and Mirror." Mahogany, fiddle back anigre, bubinga, maple, and wenge. 45" x 36" x 11".

"Nouvella Chair." Solid mahogany. The design conveys movement, counter to the usual static nature of chairs. The chair uses large through tenon joints for maximum strength at the main leg and back joints and housed mortises and tenons for the remaining joints.

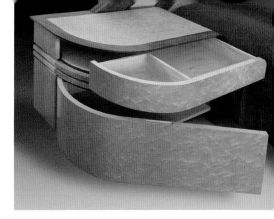

"Nightstand," drawer and door open.

"Deco Bedset." Bird's eye maple and wenge.

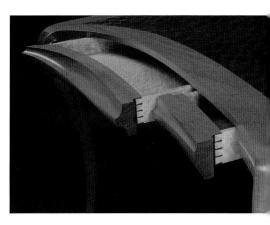

"Nouvella Desk" detail.

"Nouvella Desk." Mahogany, figured makore, and bird's eye maple. 48" x 29" x 30".

Alison J. McLennan

Oakland, California

I am drawn to making studio furniture because it fulfills my analytical need for order as well as my creative need for expression. This desire to reconcile precision and freedom is not unique to my personality. It is also a trait of our contemporary aesthetic, which I aim to contribute to in my work. Wood is approachable and easily manipulated. Thus, it is an ideal medium for me to transform a precognitive image into a resolved object. The meditative state of the craft provides me with the daily pleasure in my occupation, but the art provides me the meaning.

I believe the best art is an idea based upon knowledge and expressed with skill. It should reflect the past and hint at the future. Furniture is an intimate genre. It interacts with us by serving, stowing, cradling – supporting our bodies and our domestic activities in both personal and social ways. In doing so, studio furniture provides an intersection between design and life. I strive to make each piece express the right amount of visual information to make it art. I combine diverse materials and juxtapose lines and forms in honed proportions to build interesting, and hopefully poignant, compositions. Balancing modern and decorative, my work, like my personality, maintains a tension between ordinary and extraordinary.

With "Archerry" in cherry leather. 2010.

".Z Barstool." Maple, G-10 fiberglass, steel, lacquer, and leather.
42" x 15" x 16". 2011.

"Six-Color Coffee Table." Fiberglass, foam, plywood, pommele sapele veneer, acrylic paint, and glass.
20.5" x 47" x 24". 2009.

"Matisse's Maple." Maple, bird's eye maple, curly maple veneer, lacquer, pigmented epoxy, aluminum, and bone beads. 57" x 45.75" x 13.5". 2003.

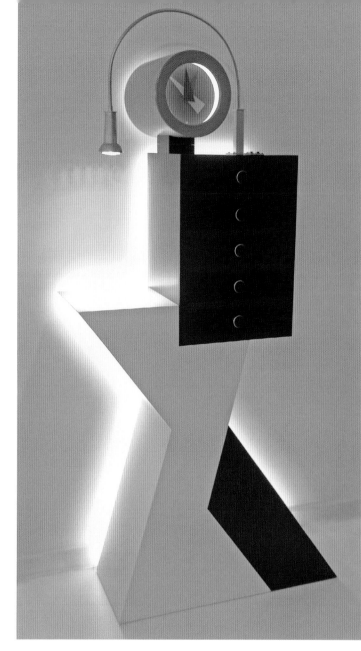

"Black + White Modern." Mahogany, plywood, Colorcore laminate, nickel-plated brass and copper, PVC, LED lights, and clock parts. 66" x 32" x 12.25". 2010.

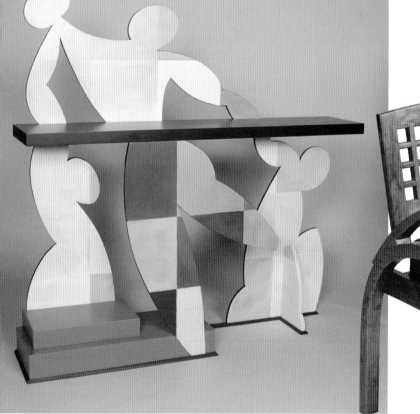

"Laocoon #1." Honduran Mahogany, plywood, fiberglass, lacquer, Formica, and 23K gold-plated brass. 70" x 51" x 16". 2002.

"Cherry Settee." Cherry, Turino leather upholstery. 31.5" x 41.5" x 24.5". 2010.

Jeff O'Brien

West Linn, Oregon

"Coopered Cabinet." Cherry, Douglas fir, and walnut. 24" x 12" x 10".

This is where something clever is written to explain the woodworker's mission and motivation. Well, I make furniture. I hope that people will like it and find it comfortable. I use traditional woodworking methods in a contemporary way, hoping that people will find it appealing. It's important to me that furniture be engaging yet practical, artistic yet useful.

My work has been described as "a new take on Modernism blending the beauty of wood with a simple geometric grace." I find my design elements in many places. I have a few styles that I prefer, as well as things I see in nature. I have also found that combining contrasting species of wood accentuates the wood as well as the design. Living in Oregon, we have some great local wood species. From walnut to Douglas fir, white oak, and western maple, there are a multitude of design possibilities. For me, building custom furniture is an adventure. I can design the piece down to the last 1/16," but in doing so, I would lose any of the opportunities that arise in the shop during construction. So my design process is somewhat casual, leaving the door open for those "design opportunities" to show themselves.

This is a second career for me. Previously, I edited video programs; they would rarely last a year – sometimes only one day. My goal is to build furniture that will last a good bit longer, more of a legacy, if you will.

"Cord Chair." Santos mahogany, ash, and Danish cord. 35" x 17" x 17".

"Signature Table." Sapele, cherry veneer, ash. Glass. 54" x 30" x 20".

"Nightstand #2." Cherry and ebonized ash. 29.5" x 20" x 15".

"Blanket Bench." Cherry and ebonized ash. 60" x 21" x 18".

Courtesy of Rebecca Nelson.

Joel Shepard

Seattle, Washington

The greatest joy I get from my work is using my creativity and curiosity to solve the everyday functional questions of a piece of furniture in a quietly elegant manner without it becoming the focal point in a room.

Japanese design seems to me the epitome of that idea. Every aspect melds function, materials, and understated elegance to create timeless, beautiful pieces of furniture and architectural details. Whenever I'm commissioned to design and build a piece, attending to the smallest of details becomes nearly a meditation on textures, materials, finishes – just the sort of things artisans of centuries past must have concentrated on to please their masters.

Since all of my work is by commission and each project is unique, I'm pleased to say that I've never done the same thing twice. Every client comes with his own set of questions setting me off on an adventure.

"Tonsu Computer Cabinet." Stained elm and traditional Japanese hardware. 54" x 48" x 24". 2010. *Courtesy of Rebecca Nelson.*

"Tonsu Entertainment Center." Dyed and stained textured elm, walnut burl, and traditional hardware. 87" x 60" x 28". 2003. *Courtesy of Rain Grimes.*

"#4 Step Tonsu." Rare SE Asian veneer, wenge, and ebony. 45" x 52" x 15". 1993.

Rich Soborowicz

Covington, Washington

"Burly Side Boy." This piece is made from Oregon black walnut burl and ebony, hence the name for the piece. The top is a 16-quarter book match pattern. The doors are a 4-quarter book match; the sides are book matched. 50" x 33.5" x 20".

Even at an early age I enjoyed working with my hands and being creative. Working with wood is challenging and rewarding to me. My woodworking hobby grew into a passion, which in turn became a profession. I have supplemented self-taught skills and artistic eye with professional training to speed up the learning and proficiency curves.

My style incorporates clean lines that produce exceptional pieces of furniture. These pieces are functional and can be considered art. My goal is to emphasize and incorporate flowing lines that are attractive, elegant, and depictive of nature. The style is based on traditional design with influence from Asian and Shaker design.

I also incorporate decorative details such as inlays and use highly figured woods. Highly figured woods have organic characteristics and what I call the wow or knockout factor. I put a great deal of care and attention into each piece and truly feel that these finished pieces are part of me, because of what I put into them. It is my desire to share my work with my client and to see how my work takes on a life of its own.

My philosophy is basic: smile and enjoy whatever you do with a passion and remember that your world is what you make of it.

"Tansu Step Chest" as dresser. Makore and maple burl bookmatched. Note how similar the drawer tiers are. 63" x 72" x 22".

"Lingerie Chest." Sides and drawer-fronts are "steamed beech," the carcass is "steamed cherry," and the doors are English elm burl four-quarter bookmatched. The drawer beading is rosewood, and the drawer sides are Eastern hard maple that are half blind dovetailed. 30" x 71" x 18.25".

"Kumiko Bookcase." Makore is used for the casework, and the dovetails are hand cut. Peruvian walnut is used for the door grates and for the negative space below the top. 30" x 50.5" x 13".

"Credenza." Bubinga and Karelian birch. Center drawers pull out for hanging folders. 61.5" x 30" x 19.5".

"Tansu Step Chest" with two "shows" sides. Highly figured Oregon black walnut. Door resawn and book matched. 49" x 56.5" x 16".

Robert Spangler

Bainbridge Island, Washington

"Ming Armchair." Walnut. 28" x 33" x 24". 1982.

Out on a limb is an exhilarating place as well as a precarious one. Working with wood is an activity that can put you into such a place. One slip of a sharp tool and a day's work may be ruined. David Pye, in his book, The Nature and Art of Workmanship, talks about the "workmanship of risk" as opposed to "the workmanship of certainty." The workmanship of certainty determines that every operation has predetermined results and is outside the control of the workman. With the workmanship of risk, the workman controls all operations, design decisions, technical considerations, and priorities with the outcome dependent upon his/her care, judgment, and dexterity.

Regardless of the risks, I have chosen this place because it satisfies an inner need. For me that need has many forms: the need to work at a human scale and pace: the need to create a new design that challenges tradition yet expands upon it; and the gratification of crafting a beautiful object that has a personality, life and art form of its own. Out on a limb is a risky place yet it also has many rewards and satisfactions. I hope they are evident in my work.

"Port Blakely Platform Bed." Walnut and spalted alder. 74" x 28" x 85". 2010.
Courtesy of Kay Walsh.

"Duet Coffee Table."
Walnut and
figured poplar.
48" x 16" x 48". 2010.

"Isho II Bedroom Chest." African mahogany and Bolivian rosewood. 54" x 45" x 22". 2009.
Courtesy of Kay Walsh.

Craig Thibodeau

San Diego, California

"Chess Table." Macassar ebony, bubinga, holly, ebony, mother of pearl, and jatoba. 27" x 27" x 32". 2008. *Courtesy of Craig Carlson.*

Having studied traditional methods of furniture-making and classical marquetry with some of today's modern masters, I am able to combine beautiful materials, premium craftsmanship, and a touch of artistry to create custom furniture of the highest caliber. I attempt to fill the basic need for functional objects with creative detailed work far exceeding expectations.

For the past few years, I have been incorporating marquetry imagery into select pieces of my furniture. Enhancing my furniture with subtle floral ornamentations allows me to combine the structural geometry of an object with the asymmetry of nature represented in flower and leaf patterns and motifs. I see the addition of decorative marquetry as a doorway into unique and exciting visual forms and more creative freedom.

The other side of my work explores the highly formal furniture of the 1920s Art Deco era, primarily work by the designer Jacques-Emile Ruhlmann. The creation of custom furniture true to the Art Deco style requires tremendous focus and discipline and is a welcome change from the more relaxed floral decorations of my marquetry furniture. To build my Art Deco furniture, I bring together luxurious materials, outstanding finishes, and precise, and highly refined veneer work.

Client involvement has been key to my work from the very beginning. Many clients commission marquetry furniture with very specific ideas in mind for the floral arrangement and its composition. Others prefer to leave me a bit more creative space to explore and see where it leads. I appreciate both methods, and each brings interesting challenges to my work.

"Maple Leaf Cabinet." Spalted maple, mahogany, curly eucalyptus, and miscellaneous marquetry woods. 34" x 16" x 42". 2010. *Courtesy of Craig Carlson.*

"Gladiola Blanket Chest." Cherry, tineo, m'futu and various marquetry veneers. 27" x 18" x 34". 2011. *Courtesy of Craig Carlson.*

"Blue Ulysses Sideboard." Wenge, ash burl, quarter sawn maple, ebony, pau ferro, boxwood, maple, poplar, holly, and ash. 48" x 18" x 36". 2007. *Courtesy of Craig Carlson.*

"Diamond Cabinet." Jatoba, madrone burl, quarter sawn maple, and quarter sawn sapele. 34" x 20" x 42". 2008. *Courtesy of Craig Carlson.*

7 International

With shield design red gum burl bed.
Courtesy of Penny Riddoch Photography.

Randy DeGraw

Maleny, Queensland, Australia

"Triptych." Integrated culture wall sculpture: Australian red cedar and huon pine. 2'3" x 4'6" (700 x 1400mm). *Courtesy of Penny Riddoch.*

I really enjoy designing and building furniture. What makes this even more fulfilling is collaborating with my clients about the design and materials. The end result is the creation of a piece of furniture that utilizes all the character and strengths of the timber to suit the client's needs and application. A client told me recently that he thought of me as a "modern day furniture maker with an artisans approach."

As a hobby, my first series of furniture was salvaging beautifully weathered grey boards from old barns in Michigan. It was not until my move to Australia in 1982 that a stack of Fraser Island satinay beams bolted me into my first woodworking business, "Creations in Time." After winning my first art award, commissions soon followed.

Although I make furniture in a variety of styles, my preferred choice is still utilizing the timber's natural edge to emphasize the organic nature of each piece. An exciting day is when I get to work with huon pine or highly figured burls. The integration of different materials can be part of any project. Gemstones, leather, and glass are just a few things that can transform a simple object into a complex statement of color and design. All of which makes each new project an individual challenge to savor.

Sharing what I do sustains my passion for creating furniture and art. Woodworking is not just what I do, it is an expression of who I am. Whether it's making a simple box or a boardroom table, every project I undertake provides the opportunity to create a lasting memento. Building it clean, strong, and elegant provides pleasure and value for generations.

"Corner Unit." Brazilian mahogany and huon pine. 4' x 1'6" x 5'3" (1200 x 500 x 1600mm). *Courtesy of Penny Riddoch.*

"Entry Doors." New Guinea rosewood with shield design. 4'7" x 7'10" (1400 x 2400mm). *Courtesy of Penny Riddoch.*

International

David Emery

Kyneton, Victoria, Australia

I like to make things – anything really, but I find that making furniture is particularly satisfying because of the variety of techniques and skills that can be applied. Some parts of the process can be so direct and quick, while for others the pace must change, time must slow down, and your commitment must be to the task at hand to the exclusion of all else.

As a furniture designer/maker, I work both to my own designs and to the designs of others. I enjoy sorting through the design possibilities, the preferred options – what's impossible from what's merely difficult. I think that this is the main strength of someone who works with materials and techniques all the time, just knowing what you can get away with. But it is also why, for me, it is important to design with others.

I think that in the early stages of the design process it is very easy to see a construction problem coming up, and then to design around it. Working to a commission means that boundaries have been set; there are specific problems to solve. I think that it is such a privilege to be able to engage with another person, as equals but with different skills, to arrive at a design, and then to bring it physically into their lives.

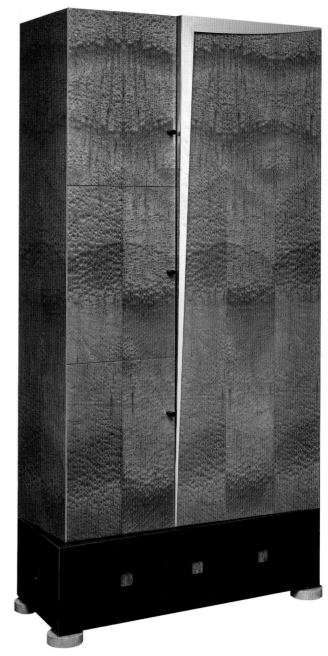

"Freycinet Cabinet." Sapele pommele and black stained poplar veneer, chrome plated brass, ebony, and ash details. 39" x 79" x 18" (2000 x 1000 x 450mm). Designed with Marcus O'Reilly. *Courtesy of John Brash.*

"Cole Cabinet." Sapele pommele and silver ash veneers, cast bronze, stainless steel wire, ebony details. 130" x 83" x 16" (3300 x 2100 x 400mm). Design: Peter D. Cole. *Courtesy of John Brash.*

"Pyramid Table." American cherry veneer on glass legs. Chrome inlay. 63" x 63" x 28.5" (1600 x 1600 x 720mm.). *Courtesy of Mark Ashkanasy.*

"Wye Table." Sycamore veneer top on wenge veneer legs. 83" x 43" x 28.5" (2100 x 1100 x 720mm). *Courtesy of John Brash.*

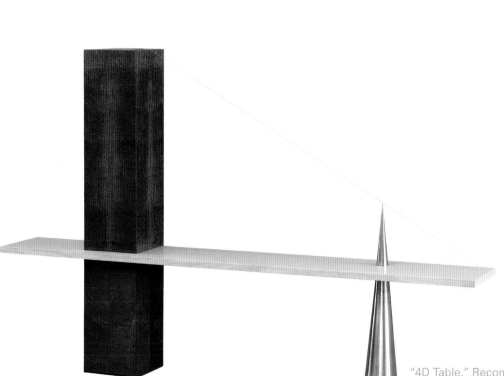

"4D Table." Reconstituted "Zebrano" veneer on painted base. 48" x 48" x 12.5" (1200 x 1200 x 320mm). *Courtesy of Big Dog Bites.*

International

Courtesy of Pam Erasmus.

Neil Erasmus
Perth, Western Australia, Australia

Unlike many designer/makers, I didn't, as a young child, have a sudden epiphany with wood. As a 10-year-old, my interests were instead focused on the eternal conundrum of life's quest. Much later, at the age of 22, my first real meeting with wood was a bit of a "blind date," as I drifted, aimlessly, from wine making into my father's furniture studio. Wood and I had a bumpy courtship in the beginning, as each doubted the other's commitment, but this situation gradually improved once marital and family commitments demanded that I settle down! So, my promise of support, together with its responsibilities, in turn, forged my bond with wood, and the first of my life's quests was answered. The "deal" was that I would breathe another life and soul into the wood; in turn, it would provide me with a living!

Philosophically, my work draws reference from the uncompromising standard of workmanship espoused by the Arts and Crafts Movement ethos, and I aspire to create it with true intellectual, cultural, and, thus, collectable value. In terms of style, I'm afraid of taking huge leaps into the abyss! My design ethos, therefore, is not about bulldozing boundaries, but instead, with "shovel in hand," I move it forward incrementally and comfortably. I like to weave a recognizable, aesthetic thread through each group of work, while maintaining a strong commitment to keeping the common-to-all-designs, technical thread as a constant. My present phase explores strong, geometric forms and fine detail, but, occasionally, I bring together two, strongly disparate flavors into the one design by juxtaposing opposites in terms of texture, shape, and color. The way light dances, prism like, with the planes and curves that make up my work helps imbue it with life and energy.

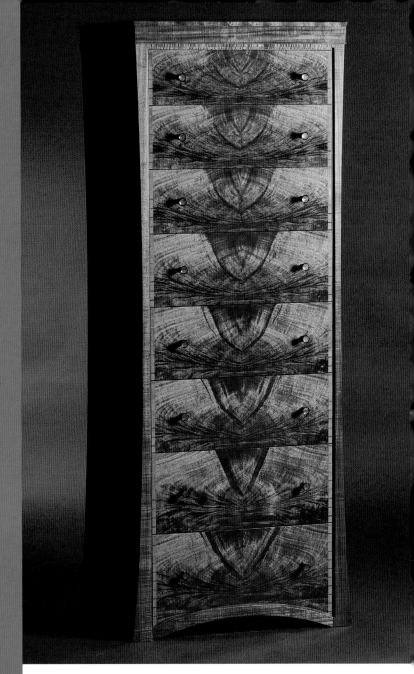

"Sylvie." Tasmanian blackwood, celery top, cedar of Lebanon, and leather. 20" x 60" x 20". 1997. *Courtesy of Evan Collis.*

"Sept Hall Table." Australian blackbutt, jarrah, camphor laurel, and leather. 51" x 35.5" x 15.75". *Courtesy of Robert Garvey.*

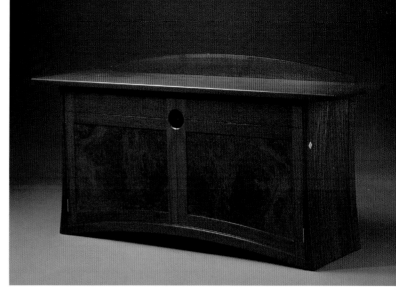

"Mantis Sideboard." Jarrah, jarrah burl, ebony, camphor laurel, and leather. 72" x 36" x 20". 1992. *Courtesy of Robert Garvey.*

"Laundry Hampers." Australian blackbutt, jarrah, and camphor laurel. 17" x 31.5" x 14". 2007. *Courtesy of Robert Garvey.*

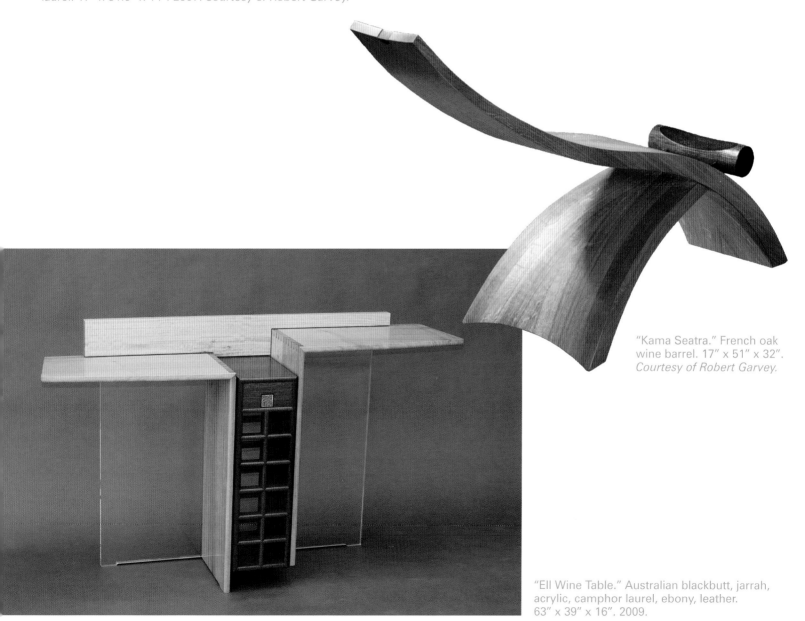

"Kama Seatra." French oak wine barrel. 17" x 51" x 32". *Courtesy of Robert Garvey.*

"Ell Wine Table." Australian blackbutt, jarrah, acrylic, camphor laurel, ebony, leather. 63" x 39" x 16". 2009.

Tracy Gumm

Sydney, NSW, Australia

I established my own studio, Irminsul, in 2007. My goal was to create contemporary, well designed furniture from wood I have personally sourced. My pieces are made using traditional techniques and possess contemporary simplicity.

The Bella Stool is a modern slant on an Arts and Crafts style stool. Perfectly suited to modern casual dining or relaxing with friends and a glass of wine. It was made soon after completing my studies and is influenced by my teacher, master craftsman Neil Erasmus (see page 170). My wine rack was the result of my exploration into laser cutting. I am interested in combining modern technologies with traditional techniques like veneering. I also enjoy creating sculptural pieces.

"Forseti Table." Yarri, blackwood, and wenge. Commissioned by a Sydney barrister, this piece showcases a special piece of blackwood salvaged from the Tasmanian wilderness. Two pieces of wenge frame the blackwood, and there is an inlay of blackwood running around the apron and legs. The rest of the table is made from yarri, a West Australian species.
80" x 29" x 44" (2 x 0.72 x 1.1m).
Courtesy of Mimi Kelly.

"Wine Rack." Blackwood and birch plywood. 20" x 26" x 7" (50 x 65 x 16cm). *Courtesy of Mimi Kelly.*

"Bella Stool." Celery pine and stainless steel footrest. 22" x 32" x 17" (55 x 80 x 42cm). *Courtesy of Mimi Kelly.*

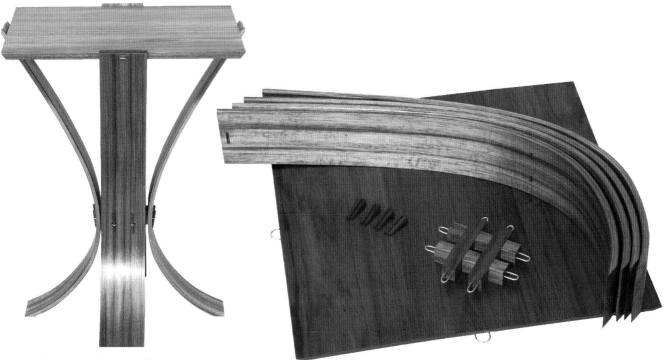

"Curly Table." Blackwood. The joinery system is a modern interpretation of the classic Arts & Craft wedges, utilizing nickel silver wire. 20" x 25" x 20" (50 x 60 x 50cm). *Courtesy of Philip Kuruvita (Web: www.Kuravita.com.au).*

"Curly Table Flatpack." Designed as flatpack concept for high end galleries, this piece won the people's choice award at the Tasmanian Wood Design Collection Biennial Exhibition in June 2006. *Courtesy of Philip Kuruvita (Web: www.Kuravita.com.au).*

International

Berto Pandolfo
Sydney, NSW, Australia

My creative journey began with my grandfather who operated a workshop in Cooma, a small country town in New South Wales, Australia. There he crafted, repaired, and restored wooden furniture. I spent a great deal of time in this workshop, ultimately acquiring an understanding of material transformation, basic mechanical concepts, and aesthetic considerations. My journey since then has remained unchanged; I am still driven by a desire to express myself through creative endeavor. I have, however, found a particular professional niche and consider myself an industrial designer operating in the context of small batch or limited run production.

If my childhood set the platform for my career, my experience as a young graduate influenced my artistic direction. I found great enjoyment and stimulation from working in large factories: places where machines and technology transformed human ideas into modern day artifacts. I have the utmost respect for the ability of a craftsperson to transform material into an object, but the singular nature of this process for me was problematic, I became absorbed by the challenge to create multiples. I am also intrigued by the partnership between a designer and machinery, I found that respect and humility in this context is not dissimilar to that that exists between a fine wood craftsperson and the material and tools that are central to his/her craft.

My practice is focused around the aim to investigate how new and emerging materials and technologies can be incorporated into innovative design solutions, and I challenge myself to bring together the opposites of manual skill and industrial automation. My interest in factories and machines drives my goal to produce objects for as broad an audience as possible.

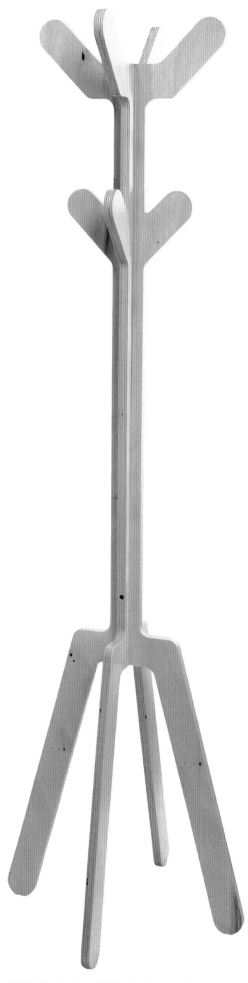

"RAK Coat-stand." Birch plywood. 20" x 20" x 67". 2002. *Courtesy of Dieu Tan Photography.*

"TAV Dining Table." Birch plywood,
71" x 29.5" x 28.5". 2005.
Courtesy of Dieu Tan Photography.

"CRM Stool/Side Table." Sheet metal,
14" x 15" x 19". 2007. *Courtesy of Dieu
Tan Photography.*

"ILT Table Light." Acrylic and aluminum. 2008. The ILT table light is the result of a
research project into cold-forming acrylic sheet. Cold-forming is the ability to create
form without the need for molds or external inputs such as heat and pressure. The
design exploits acrylic's natural characteristics of crystal-like transparency, intense
color, high gloss finish, and limited flexibility. The bottom cylindrical part serves as a
base to keep the light vertical. Since it is clear, light escapes onto the table surface.
The clear base also reduces the visual mass of the light, and a sense of weightlessness
is achieved. The top cylinder or diffuser can be produced using either opaque or
transparent acrylic, depending on what type of illumination is desired.

Henry Pilcher

Sydney NSW, Australia

"Grounded 2007." Core strength is formed by stack laminating corrugated cardboard. All weight is transferred straight to the ground through the corrugated flutes, allowing the structure to hold weights of 150kgs plus. The design incorporates fabric and ply as an attempt to make the cardboard visually acceptable by associating it with materials we already relate to in seating. *Courtesy of Dieu Tan.*

B orn in 1985, I was educated at the Australian National University and Rhode Island School of Design, majoring in furniture design. I set up my own design studio, "Henry Productions," in Sydney in 2010, and later that year was awarded with "Australian IDEA Awards: Best Emerging Designer."

I currently operate in the fields of furniture, product, and lighting design and am driven by a desire to venerate the innate qualities of base materials. Guided by a progressive approach to material choice, my designs are characterized by methods of sophistication in innovation, yet pared back and approachable in aesthetic. I draw inspiration from design history and material experimentation to create products that celebrate a marriage of craft and industrial technology.

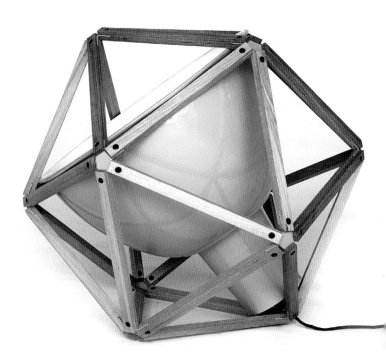

"Block 2 2009." This design turns the classic industrial lampshade into a playful, dynamic lighting feature encasing it in a geometric timber frame. The unique frame allows the light to be positioned on one of 20 bases, providing versatile light play in any room.
Courtesy of Michelle Taylor.

"Secede 2009." Most desks have a flat work surface with some sort of drawer or storage unit incorporated or near by. The concept in this piece was to separate the clutter and create surface offerings at different heights and spaces for specific items. The under frame is simply a structure propping up the laminated surfaces and protrudes in one corner to act as a support for books. Two laminated trays are embedded into the work surface to replace the act of drawers; the result offers sufficient capacity for storage without the added clutter and weight associated with conventional filing solutions. *Courtesy of Bo Wong.*

OD Chair. Designed as a side chair that can be easily packaged and transported, the OD can be dismantled into six separate components by simply removing two bolts on either side of the chair. The seat is bound by a canvas backing, which allows it to fold up like a garage roller door, while each of the chair's components is outlined with a black chamfer to highlight their individual profile.

"Three 2010." As a design almost ascetic in principle, Three is a re-think of the side table without compromising on functionality. The first of three components offers a generous and unobstructed top surface, while the minimal under frame provides for storage and arrangement of books and magazines. *Courtesy of Andrew Young.*

International

Courtesy of Andrew Lloyd.

Lex Stobie

Thebarton, South Australia, Australia

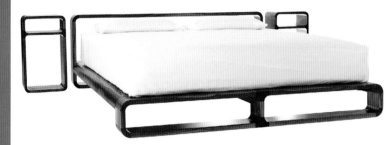

"Dela Livet (Bed)." American walnut.
7.87' x 2.29' x 6.56' (2400 x 700 x 2000mm). 2008.
Courtesy of Andrew Lloyd.

When designing a new piece of furniture, I envision the object. I then deconstruct it into the many components and their individual roles that work together to form this object. The research and development process that takes place at this point is an exciting task, and one that sometimes presents almost impossible challenges. It is the refined outcome that I seek! I desire an aesthetic solution that presents the most appropriate celebration of the chosen materials. There is a skill and an understanding that it is required in order to provide function within form. And I look for assistance in deriving these outcomes with tools like the golden ratio and a strong adherence to principles of three-dimensional designs and embellishing the negative space.

As a furniture designer, I am passionate about the impact of my practice, and nature is a truly integral feature of what I do. I therefore conduct my practice in a fashion that is deliberate and considered. I strive to create items of furniture that deliver pleasure and purpose to their recipient. My design practice emphasizes the integrity of a discerning craftsman and adopts a commitment to preserving the sensibility of my craft, connecting to future generations. I look to the environment around me for inspiration, observing forms and ideas within the naturally occurring and built environment that I can morph into new concepts. I witness the way we go about our business, inhabiting our environments, relating to hand made furniture, and appreciating its origins. My task gives me immense satisfaction!

"PPW1." American walnut, hoop pine plywood, paper and cotton. 8.20' x 8.20' x 1.97' (2500 x 2500 x 600mm). 2007. *Courtesy of Andrew Lloyd.*

"Chambers." American walnut. 7.22' x 2.43' x 3.28'
(2200 x 740 x 1000mm). 2007. *Courtesy of Andrew Lloyd.*

"Birds of a Feather." Australian blackwood. 2.95' x 1.56' x 1.31'
(900 x 475 x 400mm). 2009. *Courtesy of Andrew Lloyd.*

"Inflexion." European Oak and glass. 3.28' x 1.44'
(1000 x 440 mm). 2005. *Courtesy of Andrew Lloyd.*

International

Joram Schurmans

Ghent, Belgium

Born in an artistic family, my father a painter and my mother a classical singer, I early on developed a love for aesthetics. After studying art in school, I became an apprentice for a furniture maker in Leuven (known for the Belgian beer Stella Artois). My love affair with wood began.

After my apprenticeship, I worked for a restoration shop of antique chandeliers while making my furniture after work. I also took courses in England with Chris Arnold (cabinetmaker/restorer) to fine tune my craft. These courses opened up a whole new world of possibilities as I learned to work with hand tools. My dream was to make modern furniture with traditional techniques. Slowly, I started to design my own pieces, until I thought it was time to start my own workshop as an artisan. For this, I used the name RAM, a part of my first name "Joram" and also a classical symbol throughout history (the horns of a ram, Aries).

For me, the link between functions and materials results in pure form. The proportions of an object define its elegance. Originality, attention to details, and use of noble and qualitative materials make it an object that will age with growing beauty.

"Round Tables." Detail of a variety of round tables (bubinga, walnut, gonçalo alves). 2008.

"Bed in Loft." American walnut with two night tables made for a loft in Ghent. 2004.
Courtesy of Lieven Lefere.

"Three Nesting Tables." Santos rosewood. 2007.

Carlos Motta

São Paulo, SP, Brazil

Radar Rotating Armchair." Rediscovered (demolition) peroba rosa wood and iron. 26.4" x 26.4" x 28.3" (67 x 67 x 72cm). 2008.
Courtesy of Fernando Laszlo.

I remember the first time I was a designer. It happened in a completely intuitive way and without awareness of the process, technique, or even the aesthetic result. I was walking on a desert beach after a delirious surf session. I found a beautiful piece of drift wood brought by the sea, took it to my house – it became the first piece that I made: a bookshelf. I loved the whole process; I loved the final result. This was the impetus to make new pieces and seek the most appropriate construction techniques. It was also the impetus to seek architecture and woodworking courses.

It was a happy path, as it became clear that designing the plan and moving it to the three-dimensional, mastering the constructive technique, would be the fastest and safest way to design and build pieces for the Brazilian furniture market.

I graduated in architecture in 1976, then went to California and stayed there until 1978, learning woodworking and construction technology with wood and steel. Then I returned to Brazil and started my business, the Atelier Carlos Motta, which develops furniture prototypes, handmade furniture, special pieces, unique ones for collectors, designs for industrial production, architecture, and civil construction. Our main feature throughout these more than 35 years of work has been responsibility for environmental and social areas. I believe that there is no good design or good project if there is not the prerequisite of responsibility and respect for our planet.

"Port Manteau Mandacaru 2." Rediscovered (demolition) peroba rosa wood, aroeira wood, and cedar wood (stained). 44" x 23.6" x 93.7" (112 x 60 x 238cm). 2009.
Courtesy of Fernando Laszlo.

"CM7 Armchair." Certified sucupira wood.
29" x 28" x 30.3" (74 x 71 x 77cm). 1985.
Courtesy of Romulo Fialdini.

"Asturias Rocking Armchair." Rediscovered peroba rosa wood.
30.3" x 42.9" x 29.5" (77 x 109 x 75cm). 2001. *Courtesy of Romulo Fialdini.*

"Touch Me Not Table." Jacaranda wood, sucupira wood,
mogno wood, marfim (ivory) wood, and cabriuva wood. Made
for the Design and Nature exhibition, this table is constructed
from Amazon timber that should not be used unless certified.
Each piece of wood was shaped and pointed, resulting in an
aggressive piece. The glass top is dangerously loose, just resting
on its own weight. It is not a utilitarian piece. 35.6" x 28.9"
(90.5 x 73.5cm). 1999. *Courtesy of Romulo Fialdini.*

"Sabre Armchair." Certified sucupira wood. 27.9" x 31.5" x 32.7"
(71 x 80 x 83cm). 1993. *Courtesy of Romulo Fialdini.*

International

Jane Hall

Toronto, Ontario, Canada

This chair had wonderful bones. Inspired by the Designers Guild bold print, the frame was painted in a Kelly green, and the back was painted with a bold poppy design in contrasting pinks.

I like to think of myself as a Mistress of Color. I'm an artist and designer focusing on the use of color and pattern in the domestic environment. I love color in all its exotic richness and delight in creating objects – furniture, throws, accessories, lampshades, drapes, and cushions that create emotion, or surprise, or harmony (sometimes all three) in the observer.

Operating from Toronto, Canada, I provide color consultation and interior design services to homeowners and create an eclectic range of custom furniture and objets d'art in what has become my trademark "Jane Hall Style." Parlaying a university degree in fine art and anthropology into a 30-year career, I create hand-painted chairs – fine art canvases upon which you can sit – and reupholster classic furniture with stunning fabrics in dramatic, unexpected combinations of color and patterns. This furniture is totally unique, often made from clients' family treasures or pieces I have discovered. It is "green" with new life, and "repurposed" with five or six or more different, artfully arranged fabrics sewn or quilted together by my talented "elves" and couriered to customers the world over. As you can see, I love details and decoration, where objects exist solely to add color and humanity to our lives – the antithesis of a century of bland corporate design that has left us bereft of beauty.

This vignette at Jane Hall The Voice Of Style is a grouping of custom made products made in the Passion color group. The five color groupings in the store include Flirt, Serenity, Classic, Spice, and Passion.

Two chairs in the Classic group are in a favorite color combination: aubergine and bottle green. One is upholstered in canvas and hand painted; it is paired with a 1920s era asymmetrical carved armchair upholstered in silks and cut velvets.

This Queen Anne Cameo chair was given a modern twist with a hand painted seat using a poppy design in lively tangerine and leaf green. Two different coordinating Designers Guild silks were chosen for the front and back of the chair.

This 1880s antique Victorian settee beautifully carved with a rose was hand painted and distressed with a magenta and copper finish. I used a combination of six different Designers Guild fabrics in a combination of my favorite colors, magenta, plum, and pumpkin. Nothing is more decadent and luxurious then cut velvets and woven and embroidered silks in jeweled and regal colors.

International

Peter Wehrspann

Toronto, Ontario, Canada

"Holtzundmetal Chandelier." Aluminum and oak veneer.
6" x 7" x 30". 2005. *Courtesy of Stephen MacLeod.*

Born in Toronto, I have widened my perspective by traveling and living abroad in Japan, Switzerland, and Denmark. My work has been published in a wide variety of media and can be found in popular Toronto retail stores, entertainment establishments, and homes.

I believe good design enhances our daily lives physically and psychologically. My work is guided by the search for simple beauty and function. With a thirst for aesthetically pleasing things and what I believe is an intimate understanding of materials, I attempt to marry disparate materials with ease and grace. My approach is simple and iterative. It helps me attain my goal of contributing good design to a much deserving customer base.

I am a furniture designer, craftsman, and design researcher. After graduating from Sheridan College in Ontario, Canada, I continued my studies overseas at Danish Design School, Copenhagen. Before studying furniture craft and design, I received a degree in mass communications from Wilfrid Laurier University in Waterloo, Ontario. I am writing my thesis for a master's degree in industrial design at Carleton University. I highly value my diverse education and its affect on my work.

As founder and chief designer of Holtzundmetal. I've been developing working relationships with residential clients, interior designers, architects, musicians, and film directors. I create furniture because it gives me a sense of control, peace, and satisfaction. It is the relationships that I build and the inspiration I get from other amazing artists, athletes, and professionals that drive my work.

"Ideal Source Lounger." Reclaimed hickory.
24.5" x 28" x 27". 2006. *Courtesy of Stephen MacLeod.*

"Post Chairs." Stainless steel and reclaimed canvas CDN mailbag, c.1920. 19" x 29" x 20". 2007. *Courtesy of Stephen MacLeod.*

"WTC I'm Not Garbage Chair." FSC maple, organic fibers, and water-based ink. 25" x 34" x 19". 2008. *Courtesy of Stephen MacLeod.*

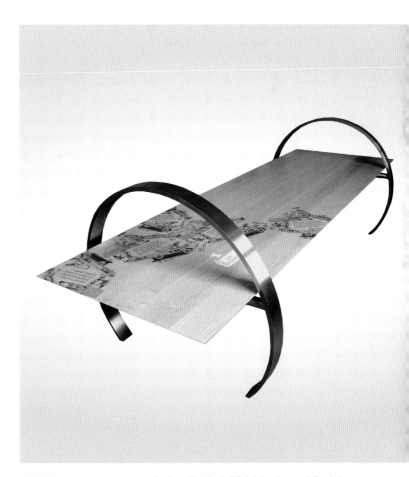

"WTC I Am Homegrown Coffee Table." FSC Maple and Stainless Steel. 20.5" x 13" x 66". 2008. *Courtesy of Stephen MacLeod.*

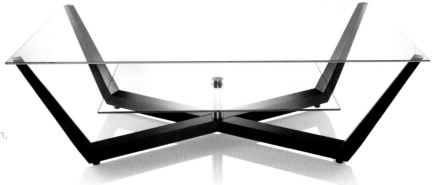

"Il Ragno Italiano." Black lacquer on maple, milled aluminum, and tempered glass. 24" x 15" x 48". 2008. *Courtesy of Stephen MacLeod.*

Guy Bucchi

Matakohe, Northland, New Zealand

"Japanese Bull." Forged steel, rivets, and manuka (NZ native wood).

To imagine, draw, and create objects is an excellent mental and physical exercise. It is also to affirm one's identity, to discover more about oneself. My furniture is the result of many years of research and my love of old hand tools (which in my heart remain unequalled in their elegance and beauty). They encourage me to create.

I make furniture because of its direct relationship with humans, less for comfort, more so for a cultural approach. Since 1988, I have been putting my ideas to paper. My drawings are spontaneous, an action, expression bringing out of the inner self what one doesn't really control.

Every design starts from an idea that we develop. My work is midway between design and art, one-off or very limited series, artisanal and made with hand tools not machines. Metal being malleable really suits my form of expression; when used with other materials (i.e., wood, rope, copper, or glass), it gives a complimentary outcome.

Movement, symmetrical or not, harmony, and space representation are globally taken into account as the object I want to represent depends on them. I suppose creating for most is very demanding, passionate, exacting, needing constant concentration, because it obliges us to give the best of ourselves all the time. It gives me pleasure to express "dreamtime" through creating, asserting my difference and continuing the tradition of "handmade." I will try to continue to make furniture until my hands become too frail to hold the tools.

"Bull." Forged steel and plywood.

"Looking for Picasso." Forged steel and kauri (NZ native wood).

"Spring." Forged steel and plywood.

"Gladiator." Forged steel and rimu (NZ native wood).

"Ocean." Forged steel and swamp kauri 5000 years old (NZ native wood).

"Hook." Forged steel and macrocarpa (NZ native wood).

International

Courtesy of Michael Thomas.

Ed Cruikshank

Arrowtown, Central Otago, New Zealand

"1821 Revolving Dining Table." One in a series of five, black walnut and gun blued steel. The table top gently tapers towards the outside to create a finely balanced edge. 71.5" x 29" (1821 x 740mm). 2011. *Courtesy of Dave Comer.*

My work is about people – family, friends, ancestors, and those as yet unborn. The best old pieces carry the marks and wear of time gone by and mingle the stories of their previous owners with those of today. No piece of furniture captures this idea more so than the dining table, one of the few remaining "soulful" gathering points in our lives. We sit around a dining table with people we love. We've gathered like this for thousands of years making it an almost sacred ritual. This particular dining table – entitled 1821 - was designed with this idea very much at its heart. Moreover, 1821 is about the very conversations that take place around that table.

I created it for an international art exhibition entitled "roundabout," featuring work by 108 contemporary fine artists from around the world. Invited to focus on the use of language, the key to human communication, I decided to emphasize miscommunication and ignorance that so often leads to conflict and war and built the table from gun-blued steel and walnut, the traditional materials of firearms.

After 25 years designing furniture – from fine cabinet making to industrial design, working alongside Viscount Linley in London for 10 years before emigrating to the alpine region of New Zealand's South Island – the "roundabout" commission cemented my belief in the seamless continuum of artisan to artist. Great design works in the same way as great art, music, poetry or indeed the perfection of nature. It is intuitive and powerful, obvious yet mysterious. Ultimately, the best work – work that melds the highest caliber of creativity, craftsmanship and design – endures. Like a great story, it links and enriches lives across many generations.

Timber segments draw the eye towards the central gun blued steel hub. *Courtesy of Dave Comer.*

The underside. *Courtesy of Dave Comer.*

Each floating solid timber segment represents one of 108 artists featured in the *roundabout* exhibition. They float as individual pieces, independent entities that come together to create a resilient yet flexible whole. *Courtesy of Dave Comer.*

Indented Braille in the centre of the table quotes Martin Luther King Junior: *"I have decided to stick with love, hate is too great a burden to bear."* The word *"love'"* remains stationary as the table turns. *Courtesy of Dave Comer.*

With Spacejunk. 2005. Courtesy of Daniel Allen
Web: www.danielallen.co.nz

Mike Hindmarsh

Nelson, New Zealand

I am a New Zealand-based designer working mainly in timber – both solid wood and plywood panel product. I enjoy the crossover between art and design that furniture making can provide. Objects that are both functional and beautiful! I specialize in large-scale outdoor furniture and design for civic and corporate environments. My designs are created to enhance the public environment, both functionally and aesthetically. I work with the client to create a design that is purposefully built for specific environments incorporating materials of the client's choice. I have work in public and private collections in New Zealand and internationally.

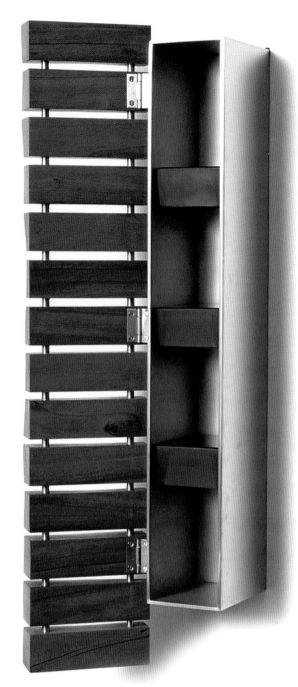

"Ebb Wall Cabinet." Rata, stainless steel, and cast glass. 8" x 30" x 9". 2006.

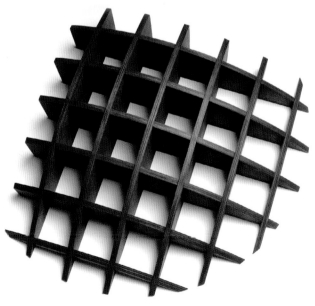

"Babyspacejunk." Plywood and stain. 22" x 22" (550 x 550mm). 2008.

"LVL (laminated veneer lumber) Lounge Chair." 27" x 30" x 28" (700" x 800" x 730mm). 2011. *Courtesy of Jeanie Robertson.*

"Space Junk Sidetable." Toughened glass and stained plywood. 20" x 22" x 22" (500 x 550 x 550mm). 2008. *Courtesy of Daniel Allen Web: www.danielallen.co.nz.*

"Flat Packable Stool and Table." Plywood and paint. Table: 27" x 52" x 30" (700 x 1330 x 770mm); stool 16" x 18" x 12" (400 x 450 x 300mm). 2010.

*Courtesy of Glenn McLelland,
Web: www.supersharpshooter.co.nz.*

David Kirkland

Wellington, New Zealand

"Georgian panel room study." New Zealand kauri.
*Courtesy of Glenn McLelland,
Web: www.supersharpshooter,co.nz.*

Some things cannot be rushed. Restoring and creating furniture is one of them. For a cabinet maker in 1964, 10,000 hours was the duration of an apprenticeship. I completed such an apprenticeship at the distinguished William Nees & Sons in Dunedin and came away with a superb knowledge of the art of cabinet making – both in constructing and restoring. I spent time in London (working for Roger Board & Son) using the traditional methods to create eighteenth century style period rooms.

I set up business in Wellington, New Zealand, in the early 1980s. Constructing an impeccable piece brings great satisfaction and pride. The challenge of designing a piece from pattern to end product, seeing how the joints will become one, drawing the piece out in scale and putting hours of physical effort into crafting and perfecting the wood is a labor of love. I have a keenness about furniture, about the way it should feel and fit like an intricate puzzle. The challenge is manifest – miss one measurement and the piece is lost.

"Regency Rosewood Demi-Lune" (reproduction). Pernambuco with ebony stringing & New Zealand holly with detail of marquetry (drawer). *Courtesy of Glenn McLelland, Web: www.supersharpshooter,co.nz.*

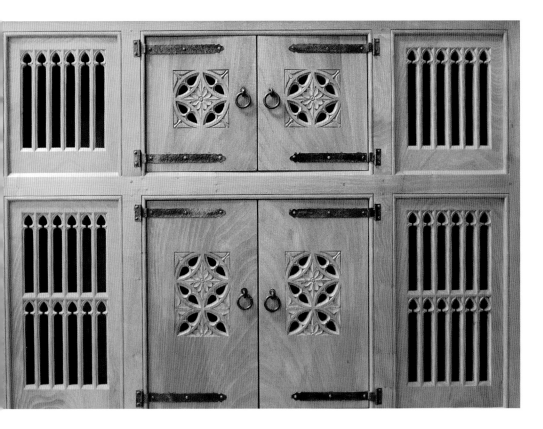

Sixteenth Century Gothic Hutch
(reproduction). Carved chestnut.
Courtesy of Glenn McLelland,
Web: www.supersharpshooter,co.nz.

International

William Acland
Cambria, England

After studying three-dimensional design and furniture making followed by three years in the industry, I soon realized that my real interest was in "real furniture." With the experience I gained and with an understanding of the principles of good design and making, I decided "to design and make furniture without compromise; original designs that are not concerned with passing trends… furniture that will endure and be cherished by its owner."

I am now a partner in Waters & Acland, a business that specializes in hand crafting beautiful and perfectly made furniture. As one of a team of four and the head designer, I like to stay hands on in the workshop, enabling me to retain an affinity with the material the designs are to be made from… wood: English oak, perhaps the hardest and most majestic of the oaks, often traditionally quarter sawn (I aim to select only the finest examples of this beautiful timber); ash, a diverse and flexible timber often demonstrating dramatic, tightly packed figure bands, "ripple ash" and dark heartwood "olive ash;" English cherry, close grained, silky and warmer in tone than oak or ash; and cedar of Lebanon with its seductive aroma. Native elm, sycamore, and walnut are also some of the woods I use.

Every commission is unique, like the clients and their needs. By understanding their needs, I endeavor to design pieces that meet clients' exact requirements, resulting in furniture that is made with exceptional materials and meticulous craftsmanship.

"Hack Chest." Oak, rosewood, and cedar of Lebanon. 42" x 20" x 61". 2010.

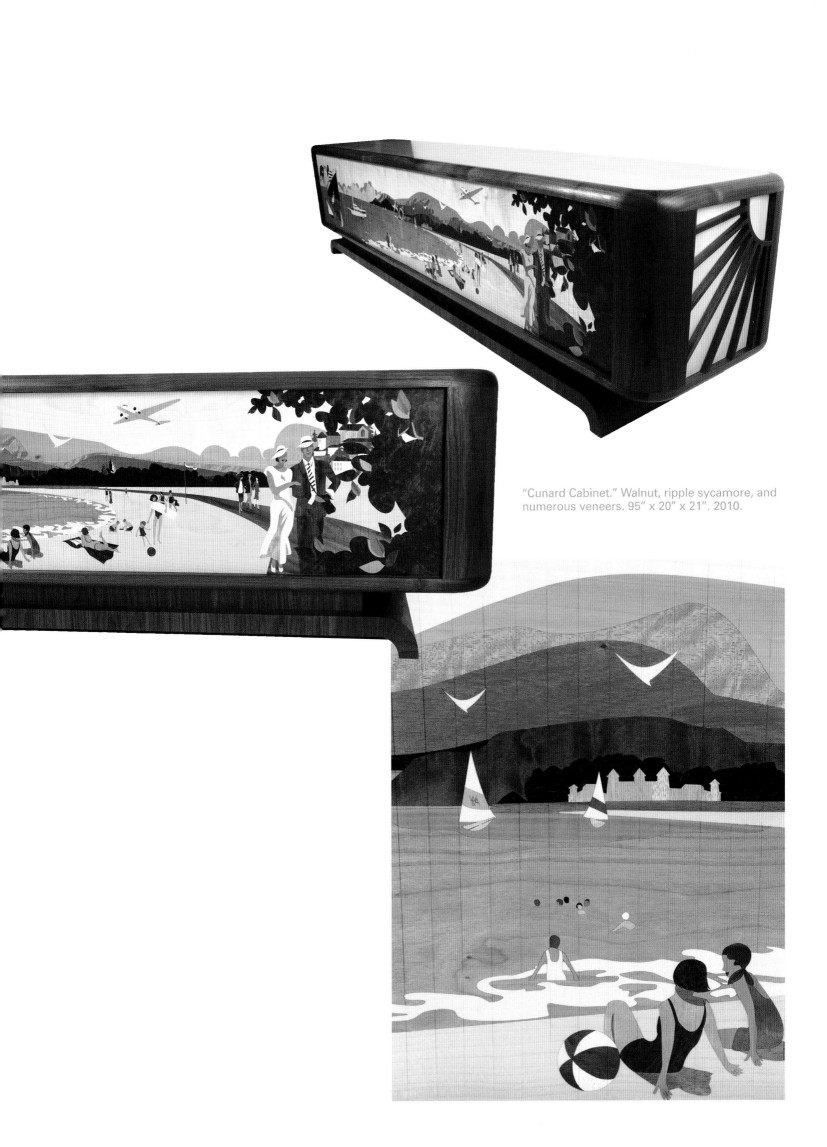

"Cunard Cabinet." Walnut, ripple sycamore, and numerous veneers. 95" x 20" x 21". 2010.

Joe della-Porta

East Sussex, England

"Kyoto Desk." High gloss sprayed side table/desk. 18" x 59" x 32". (45 x 150 x 65cm). 2011.

My furniture design is really a story of "East meets West," as I am totally inspired by the refinement of Japanese craftsmanship and the unique way this can fuse with Western culture. I have always admired the discipline and simplicity of Japanese art and design. After training as a carpenter and joiner, I traveled to Japan to study the art of traditional Japanese house building. Subsequently, I was awarded a place to study at the world-renowned Parnham College, run by John Makepeace. After graduating in 1996, I established "della-Porta design."

Coming from an Italian family of artisans, I also draw on the disciplines of my two brothers: one a US-based sculptor and the other a UK-based industrial product design engineer, to create unique pieces which blend natural and man-made materials. These qualities shine through each commission, which is then brought further to life by adding a reflection of my client's personality. I strive to create something unique and extraordinary every time and am passionate about challenging my client's brief so the finished piece exceeds his/her expectations. For me, the excitement and satisfaction lies in creating work with an inherent presence that I know will be cherished and looked after for years to come.

"Jupiter Coffee Table." Solid and veneer wenge with camphor burr. 32" x 32" x 18". 2011.

"Sumo Chair." Solid European oak. 28" x 31" (back) x 16". 2010.

"Jarrah Burr." A sculptural side table. Solid jarrah burr (Australian) and acrylic. 20" x 15" x 16". 2010.

"Karma. A Butsudan." Laminated and sprayed board material and solid oak with gold leaf interior. 23" x 28" x 13". 2009.

International

Paul Gower

Dorset, England

My approach to furniture design is brilliantly encapsulated in the words of the great architect Voysey: "simplicity requires perfection in all its details, whilst elaboration is easy in comparison."

"Cube Boxes." Ash, oak, and maple. In order to hide the inner space, the lid is disguised by matching the grain across the gap and around the sides.
12" x 12" x 12" (0.3 x 0.3 x 0.3m).
Courtesy of Mike Murless Photography.

"Sigmoid Table." English ripple ash and stainless steel. This 8-10 seat dining table draws its inspiration from naturally occurring shapes in rocks. Three slits in the top give the impression of a torn apart surface. Tubular stainless steel complements the dining chairs and provides a sinuous visual dynamic. 87" x 29" x 47" (2.2 x 1.2 x 0.73m). *Courtesy of Mike Murless Photography.*

"Hide and Squeak Jewelry Cabinet." Stainless steel, wenge, and maple. The cabinet comprises 86 solid stainless steel cubes stacked around a nine-drawer wenge cabinet. To add an element of intrigue, a magnetic key is used to open the drawers.

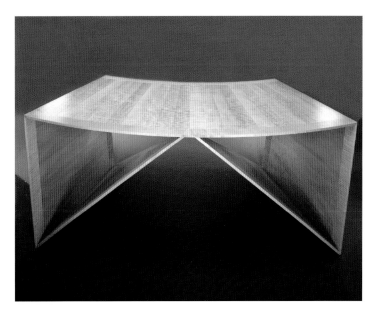

"Origami Desk." English ripple sycamore. Stunning bookmatched veneers fan out from the center to provide a rich three-dimensional dynamic effect. 67" x 29" x 32" (1.7 x 0.8 x 0.73m). *Courtesy of Mike Murless Photography.*

"Sandwave Chest of Drawers." American brown ash and aluminum. Drawer sides and carcass are mitred to produce a sharp clean outline. Aluminum handles float within a letterbox groove. 55" x 30" x 16" (1.4 x 0.4 x 0.76m).

Courtesy of John Andow Widgery Studios.

Harry Hare

North Devon, England

I strive to give my clients years of fulfillment every time they look at my furniture. My main goal is to exceed their expectations and try to make something that will be treasured for many generations. I am equally happy making for a local client as I am for a client on the other side of the world, believing that bespoke furniture should be attainable for all.

I take inspiration from the natural environment, be it cornfields ebbing and flowing or staggering rock formations found on nearby beaches. One of the things I love to do is to walk around the fields and beaches taking photographs of the beautiful landscapes, which can later be referred to as a source for creativity. My furniture designs aim to be timeless and beautiful, sometimes even cool. I am now considered one of the leading designer makers in the UK.

I work on my own, with a farm dog for company, and I call on other woodworkers when needed. My workshop is on an old diary farm, and the gently rolling Devon countryside and livestock surround it. A wood-burning stove heats my workshop throughout the winter months. It gives me great satisfaction, knowing that the useless off-cuts can be utilized for warmth.

"Goliath Table." Wenge and walnut veneer. Seats 12-14. 157" x 39" x 30".

"Munro Chair and Footstool." Ash and leather. 46" x 39" x 32" and 18" x 18" x 14". *Courtesy of Rod Gonzales, Optimo Images.*

"Map Collector's Cabinet." English walnut, sycamore, and 1000 year-old yew. 35" x 25" x 9". *Courtesy of John Andow Widgery Studios.*

"Cherry Bedside Tables." Cherry, sycamore, walnut, and 1000 year-old yew. 24" x 16" x 16".

Alun Heslop
Sussex, England

It is one thing to have an idea in one's mind of a form or shape through a sense of movement; it is another thing altogether to be able to translate that concept into a manifest reality within a functional object such as a chair or bench seating piece. Visualizing the shaping cuts necessary as a series of layers is the key in order to produce the formwork. Each layer of carving and hollowing cuts becomes an integral part of the process that turns a fluid thought into a flowing line weight.

Much of the structure and shaping that goes into these works is inspired by dynamic movement through space at varying speeds, over landscape, through water, and in air – both as participator and observer such as the shape of a bike ride through mountainous terrain, the sense of wind blowing sculpting sand dunes, or the way water carves a canyon.

I set up "chaircreative" in 2006, which has produced work for both public spaces and private clients.

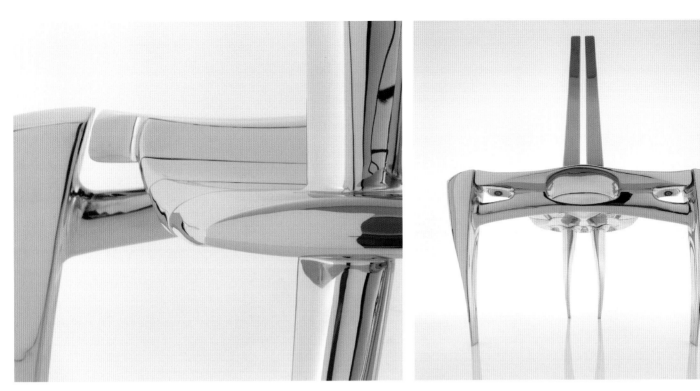

"Hammerhead RVS." Mirror polished, semi-hollow, cast stainless steel. 31.49" x 53.15" x 29.53" (800 x 1350 x 750mm). 2011. *Courtesy of Sylvain Deleu.*

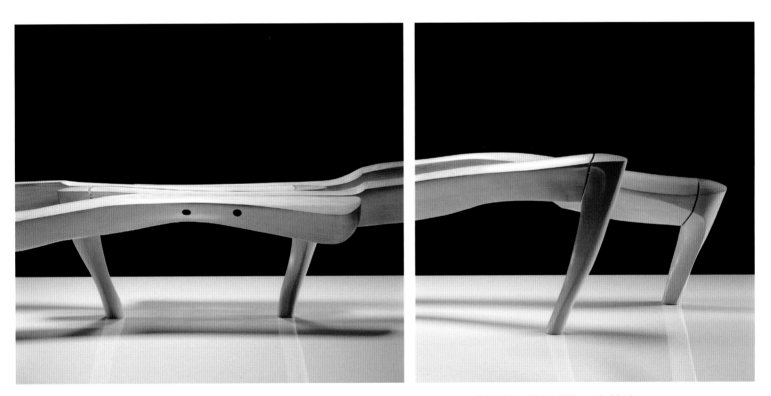

"Insictor." Carved bleached ash wood and stainless steel. 145.67" x 33.46" x 33.46" (3700 x 850 x 850mm). 2010. *Courtesy of Michael Harvey.*

Rachel Hutchinson

Wiltshire, England

I was drawn to wood from an early age, and throughout secondary school I spent an hour every day at woodwork club. I was inspired by the studio furniture of the 1970s Craft Revival, and I went on to study furniture design at university and working as an apprentice in the studio workshops of some of the UK's leading artist and craft workshops.

I decided I would produce a body of work, speculatively. I wanted to forge my own aesthetic. Shape and form are key to my ideas, but I am also keen that my furniture is functional and ergonomic to its simplest expression, a design statement that has clarity and impact. I combine sculptural ideas and utility. I use detailing to add flair and hold the piece together – everything must relate to the piece as a whole. I often develop full-scale models as part of the design process. Proportion is important, and seeing prototypes in the round, in relation to the human scale, and in the context of the room in which it will live, helps me to hone an idea.

My aspiration is to create a legacy of pieces that are unique, innovative, and exquisite. I think it is important to transcend the homogenous and commercial straitjacket by which so many twenty-first century objects are created and allow pleasure and art to rule. For this reason, I have always held "furniture making" as a commercial entity at arm's length and embraced my own foray into furniture, through exhibitions and patrons.

"Library Chair." Steam bent ash with swivel mechanism and gas lift. 45.6" x 23.6" x 23.6" (1160 x 600 x 600mm). 2009. *Photo by Andy Pinscher.*

"Telescopic Table." English ripple sycamore, block laminated with telescopic rise and fall mechanism. Height can be set at 13.7, 21.6, and 29.5" (350, 550, and 750mm); diameter is 59" (1500mm). 2008. *Photo by Andy Pinscher.*

"Zero x Wall Cabinet." Sycamore, gold leaf, gold plated brass, and convex mirror. 47.2" x 23.6" x 23.6" (1200 x 600 x 150mm). 1998. *Photo by Peter Benson.*

"Pedestal Table." Steam bent ash with plywood stained panels and burr oak. 35.4" x 17.7" x 17.7" (900 x 450 x 450mm). 1995. *Photo by Dominic Harris.*

"Cocktail Cabinet." English oak with hand blown glass panels, stainless steel bezels, silver plated latch and hinges, and toughened glass shelves. 58.2" x 25.6" x 20.5" (1480 x 650 x 520mm), 2001. *Photo by Marlborough Photo.*

International

Derrick Ibbott

Norfolk, England

"Form Coffee Table." English walnut.
47.24" x 23.62" x 19,68" (1200 x 600 x 500mm). 2006.
Courtesy of Ken Adlard.

I make furniture because I love it; have always loved it and don't know how to do anything else. Working with wood has consumed me ever since I was a little boy, leaving no time for anything else; without wood I would be lost.

My work reflects the characteristics I admire most in people: honest, solid, and well made. I enhance that foundation with curves and silky smooth finishes, making something that is strong and beautiful to look upon and a pleasure to touch. I aim for perfection, however, in this department I cannot succeed as you can keep improving things forever.

The joy of the work for me is the challenge of figuring out how to make something no matter how impossible it may seem. I always say yes to a client's request and then figure out how to make it later. This keeps the work interesting and exciting. Once I have made a piece of furniture, the satisfaction of seeing the finished piece and the appreciation of the client are well worth all the effort.

When people ask me what is your inspiration, I find it a difficult question to answer. There isn't usually anything specific that suddenly makes my brain go ding. Ideas are constantly seeping into my subconscious from daily life. I have moments in my workshop when I suddenly have to draw something out on a scrap of paper, which is just how my olive ash chest of drawers, "Symphony No 1" began. This piece later went on to receive the prestigious Claxton Stevens Award for best bespoke guild mark.

"Window Seats." Papua New Guinea rosewood.
47.24" x 29.92" x 12.60" (1200 x 760 x 320mm). 2007.
Courtesy of Ken Adlard.

"Symphony No.1." Olive ash and wenge. 59.05" x 36.50" x 18.90" (1500 x 927 x 480mm). 2009. *Courtesy of Ken Adlard.*

"Twist Table and Chairs." Brown oak. 72.44" x 45.67" x 29.92" (1840 x 1160 x 760mm). 2010. *Courtesy of Ken Adlard.*

Robert Kernohan

Antrim, North Ireland

I started making furniture nine years ago to relieve the stress associated with my profession as a surgeon. I attended a few specialist courses, but I am essentially self-taught. I enjoy working with my hands to make objects and previously built racing cars. Having always been practical, I have never been excited by intellectual pursuits. I believe that effort expended must result in tangible objects that can be appreciated by all.

I realized that if I continued working I would never reach my potential as a woodworker, so I retired early in order to devote more time to my craft. It is difficult to become known when starting out. I have been lucky in having a small group of loyal customers who appreciate fine furniture and have commissioned several pieces.

I find the variety of wood species fascinating, each different and beautiful in its own way. Each board is different from the next and can only have one ideal use, requiring care and understanding to get the best out of it. The process of exploring what the customer wants, the functionality of the piece, defining the joinery and finally the making, turning a rough board into something which is beautiful to look at and sensuous to touch excites me. Of course, each new piece is a challenge, which is often a bit scary to start with. When the commission is complete and my customer is happy, however, there can be no other endeavor more worthwhile. I believe that wood is such a precious and diminishing resource that it is our duty to make beautiful enduring things from it so that the tree may live again as furniture.

There is something magical in making. When people look at my work, it requires no description, no explanation, it stands there. It speaks for itself.

"Bar Stool." Black walnut, ebony, oil, and wax. 22" x 21" x 41". 2010.

"Conjoined Stool."
Black walnut, ebony, oil, and wax.
62" x 21" x 40". 2009.

"Rocking Chair." Ash, walnut, ebony, and osmo
oil. 28" x 42" x 43". 2011.

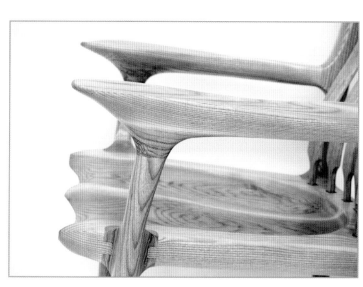

"Rocking Chair." curly maple, walnut, ebony, and osmo oil.
26" x 41" x 40".

Nicholas Langan

Cornwall, United Kingdom

Furniture in its many forms is so interactive, so essential to our lives, and challenging to get right both in its design and making. I am inspired to create furniture that reflects my surroundings, has clean lines, and employs simple decoration. It's really satisfying to know that, at Journeyman Furniture, I am adding to culture, sociology, and history, designing artifacts to be enjoyed by future generations. The knowledge that I am upholding traditional skills, but at the same time pushing forward new ideas, merging design, craft, art, and technology, excites me.

I find the commissioning experience rewarding for all involved. The client's needs and personality are reflected in my design, which ensures that the finished article enhances their environment and life. It's fantastic to be able to respond to each individual job and involve the customers so that they can truly personalize their living space.

As the designer, I do my best to get the most out of the grain, patterns, and texture of the timber. Throughout an assignment, I am in touch with the materials, using my hands to feel and my eyes to assess every component from the initial selection of timber to the final finishing.

"Footprint Occasional Table." Oak. With underside detail. 47" x 27.5" x 16.5". 2009. *Courtesy of Andrew Hawker Photography.*

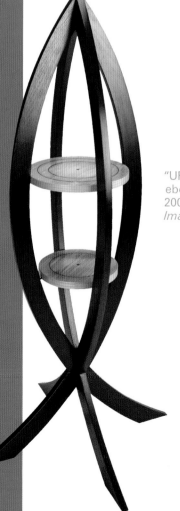

"UFO-OFU Stand." Ebonized ash, ash, ebony, and rosewood. 51" x 14" x 14". 2008. *Courtesy of Peter Phelan - The Imaging Company Ltd.*

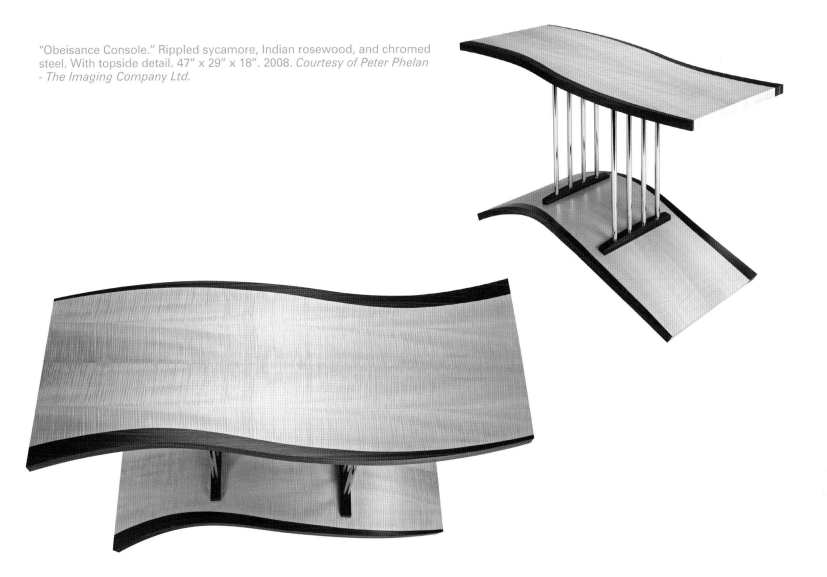

"Obeisance Console." Rippled sycamore, Indian rosewood, and chromed steel. With topside detail. 47" x 29" x 18". 2008. *Courtesy of Peter Phelan - The Imaging Company Ltd.*

"Ribbon Chair." Cherry and stainless steel. 44" x 18" x 18". 2009.
Courtesy of Andrew Hawker Photography.

Amanda Ransom

Oxfordshire, England

"English Oak Dresser c 1900." Hand carved cornice, restored and traditionally hand painted.

My English Furniture Workshop was born through my desire to restore interesting and beautiful period furniture. I find late nineteenth and early twentieth century English furniture and sympathetically restore and hand paint it in order to ensure its continued use and appreciation. I leave natural oak unpainted where possible as I believe that it is the combination of natural wood and subtle color that makes painted furniture so beautiful. Ecological issues are paramount within my restoration process. My materials and paint are eco-friendly, and all of the furniture is hand sanded.

My philosophy is about a return to furniture that is handmade and individual, away from the mass produced. I believe that the versatility and beauty of hand painted furniture have given antique and vintage furniture a new aesthetic and a chance to remain a major contributor to the success of today's more modern interiors.

In my 20s, I studied Product Design at Goldsmiths College, University of London, and went on to earn a master's degree at Central Saint Martin's College of Art and Design. At Goldsmiths, my thesis was based on the principles of "green" design and looked at the importance of aesthetics or "style" when producing environmentally conscious products that will appeal to the consumer. Eco design has since become more widespread and influential; however, new materials and methods of production tend to take priority over recycling and re-using. My MA re-enforced my belief that my desire was not to design for mass manufacture, but to try to influence the way we look at our existing items and find ways of retaining elements of craftsmanship and tradition within our ever changing environment.

"Arts and Crafts Oak Dresser c.1910." Hand forged iron work and original leaded door. Hand painted and restored with color taken from William Morris designs.

"Victorian Pembroke Table" with long drawer. Hand painted in Farrow and Ball's "Folly Green." Painting the drawer adds a "clean modern twist."

"Vintage English Linen-fold Blanket Chest." Oak. The linen-fold design dates from the fourteenth century.

The Pendulum Shift:
A Renewed Passion for the Handcrafted: As Seen Through the Eyes of a Gallerist

Lewis Wexler

I have been in the "Art Business" for many years, and the one saying I hear time and time again is that the pendulum always shifts. Tastes change and what is out of vogue will at sometime in the future be back in vogue. This applies to fashion, music, literature, and, yes, even craft and design. It seems that from the 1990s into 2000, handcrafted "studio furniture" had lost its luster with the public. Collectors gravitated toward new materials, slick new designs, and Eurocentric designers. The days of the Peter Joseph Gallery seemed to be long forgotten. Many were claiming it was the death of the studio furniture movement. I was right there in the middle of the fray, giving studio furniture its last rights. But was the death of studio furniture greatly exaggerated?

Perhaps the field of handcrafted furniture had simply changed. There are still many talented craftspeople making wonderful pieces and there are still art fairs and craft shows displaying work. One of the biggest changes is that there are fewer galleries like Peter Joseph showing the work. Pritam and Eames are still doing an outstanding job showing work, but I can list the number of galleries showing traditional studio furniture on one hand. The big question is why are there fewer galleries showing work by some of the most accomplished makers working in the field today, as opposed to the 90s when there were a number of galleries showing the work. I think the answer to that question largely rests with the artists themselves and the way furniture has been marketed and sold throughout the years.

Generally, most furniture makers tend to create work on a commission basis. This allows the maker to work closely with the client. Once the relationship between the client and the maker is established, the temptation for the maker to work directly with the client and bypass the gallery can be set in motion. Galleries tend not to want competition for sales with their own artists. If artists feel that the gallery cannot create enough sales to support them, the end result can be the breakdown of the artist/gallery relationship. So the old paradigm of the artist/gallery erodes, leading to fewer galleries showing the work and generally less public exposure. The end result is a declining interest from new collectors and the media.

However, with the advent of the Internet, an increase in art fairs, and a strong interest in the designer/maker, the field of handcrafted furniture as well as ceramic, glass, jewelry, and textile has changed and is still changing. Websites like ETSY have given rise to a new breed of maker, more hipster than hippy. A maker now has the ability to showcase their work on this site and many others like it. It allows the maker to reach a younger audience and reach potential clients on an international level. This form of marketing is still in its infancy, but as this younger generation gets older and obtains more disposable income, the Internet will be a viable sales tool for work at a higher price point.

The studio furniture movement originally developed as a reaction to the Industrial Revolution. Perhaps the new generation is reacting to the information age. In a time when mass production and disposable products are the norm, a younger audience concerned with the environment seems to be gravitating toward items that are made with sustainable materials. They also appear to take an interest in work that has a certain amount of preciousness and warmth. All social indicators point to an increased interest in the handcrafted.

Many craft shows and art fairs are available for both new and established makers to showcase their work. Craft shows have always been a traditional venue for handcrafted objects. Some of these shows have seen a decrease in attendance, but they are all in the process of finding a younger, affluent crowd. Once they figure a way to re-brand themselves, opportunities for makers will follow.

As for the established makers from the days of Peter Joseph, some have reinvented themselves, some have continued to work as they always have, and others have stopped making. They will always have a place in the history of studio furniture movement. Slowly, some pieces have entered the secondary market, some pieces fetching close to six-figure prices at auction. Many works are selling at design auctions alongside the top designers in the world.

The world of craft is in a transitional stage. There is a blurring of the lines that separate craft, art, and design, and the word "design" is largely responsible for this change. Many of today's designers are still very much craftspeople, just using newer tools to create work, such as CAD, Rhino, or Rapid prototyping. They are using the technology available to them in the design process, but are still creating the work in traditional handcrafted methods that have been used for centuries. These makers are producing exciting, conceptual, and well-crafted work, which has proven to be relevant in today's market place. It can be seen at galleries around the world, as well as design/art fairs such as Design Miami and Design Basel. Perhaps moving forward, the traditional "furniture maker" needs to be seen in a different way, as the "designer/maker." Then we will continue to see the slow shift of the pendulum toward the handcrafted.

Lewis Wexler began his career in the arts in the late 1980s as Assistant Vice President of 20th Century Decorative Arts at Christie's auction house in New York City. Following his work at Christie's, Lewis worked with world-renowned French Art Deco dealer Anthony Delorenzo at his Madison Avenue gallery. He has lectured extensively throughout the United States at institutions, including The Smithsonian's Renwick Gallery, The Furniture Society Conference, UBS's "Annual Global Media & Communications Conference," and "SOFA Chicago" (Sculptural Objects Functional Art fair). He has been featured in various national publications and appeared on the cover of Art & Antiques magazine in October 2005. Committed to the promotion of finely crafted work that pushes the perception of art, craft, and design, Lewis has also been on the jury to select work for important exhibitions throughout the United States.

Wexler Gallery opened in 2000 in the historic district of Old City, Philadelphia. Since then, the 5,600 square foot gallery has proudly showcased extraordinary work by both master artists and the emerging talent of today.

Bibliography, Accolades, and Honors

Tom Calhoun

Caldwell, Brian. "Woodworking in Paradise," *Woodshop News*. May 2009. pp. 26-29.

Hemachandra, Ray and John Grew Sheridan. *500 Cabinets: A Showcase of Design and Craftsmanship*. Asheville, NC: Lark Crafts. 2010.

Shafto, Tiffany DeEtte, and Lynda McDaniel. *Contemporary Hawaii Woodworkers*. Mountain View, Hawaii: Contemporary Publications. 2009.

Snyder, Jeff. *Wood Art Today 2*. Atglen, PA: Schiffer Publishing. 2010.

Stein, Michael. "Carving Out a Life on Maui," *Maui News*. Sept. 30, 2001. p. D1.

"For the Love of Wood," *Maui No Ka Oi*. Spring 2003. p. 79.

"Maui Woodworker Making His Mark." *Maui News*, Sept. 21, 2002. p. C1.

Time Coleman

"Applied fretwork adds color and texture." *Fine Woodworking Magazine*. Oct. 2010. pp. 84-87.

"Carving Out A Niche." *Boston Globe Magazine*. Feb 3, 2008, pp. 12-13.

Fine Woodworking Furniture: 102 Contemporary Designs. Newtown, CT: Taunton Press. 2008.

"Tim Coleman, It's all in the details." *American Woodworker Magazine*. June/July, 2009, pp. 24-27

Stephen Courtney

Fitzgerald, Oscar. *Studio Furniture of the Renwick Gallery*. Fox Chapel. 2007.2008. pp. Foreword; 70 -71.

Snyder, Jeff. *Wood Art Today 2*. Atglen, PA: Schiffer Publishing, 2010. pp. 41-43.

Michael Daniel

Arnstein, Barbara. "The Iron Man." *Ins & Outs LIC Magazine*. Fall 2005: 36-37.

Dybwad, Barb. "The Mar. of Time: The Robot Flip Clock." *Engadget*. Engadget. 26 Mar. 2005. Web.

Long Island City: Connecting the Arts. New York: Design Trust for Public Space, 2006.

McMasters, Kelly. "Shop Class." *Metrosource*. Jun.-Aug. 2002.

Nosé, Michiko Rico. *New York Artists Backstage*. Tokyo: Graphic-sha Publishing Co. Ltd. 2006.

Randy DeGraw

Burrows, Art. *The Australian Woodworker*. No. 139. June 2008.

Clayton, Pauline. *Australian Wood Review*. Interwood Holdings. June 2000. #27.

Green, Elaine, ed. *Earth Dreams Magic*. Australia: Tien Wah Press. 2010.

Mark Del Guidice

"Brush with Genius..." *Niche Magazine*. Winter 2006.

"Craft Transformed, Program in Artisanry." Fuller Craft / UMass Dartmouth.

"Framing Success." *Woodshop News*, Feb. 2006

"Furniture Makers Exploring Digital Technologies." Furniture Society. 2005.

Furniture Studio One, Furniture Society, 1999.

Hemachandra, Ray, and Craig Nutt. *500 Chairs: Celebrating Traditional & Innovative Design*. Ashland, NC: Lark Books. 2008.

Hemachandra, Ray, and John Grew Sheridan. *500 Cabinets: A Showcase of Design and Craftsmanship*. Asheville, NC: Lark Crafts. 2010.

Lark Book. *Penland Book of Woodworking*. Lark Books, Sterling Publishing. 2006.

"Sit up & Take Notice." Smith College Museum of Art, Northampton, MA.

Skinner, Tina. *Studio Furniture, Today's Leading Woodworkers*. Atglen, PA: Schiffer Publishing Ltd. 2009.

Snyder, Jeff. *Wood Art Today 2*. Atglen, PA: Schiffer Publishing. 2010.

"Tradition in Contemporary Furniture." Furniture Society, 2001.

Awards & Accolades

2011 Award of Excellence. CraftBoston, Boston, MA.

2006 Juror's Award, Crafts National. Lancaster Museum of Art, PA.

2005 Gold Award. Smithsonian Craft Show, Washington, D.C.

2005 Niche Award. *Niche Magazine,* Baltimore, MD.

2000 Artist Award [Addesso Furniture Award] Society of Arts & Crafts, Boston, MA.

2000 Marc Harrison Award Providence Fine Furniture Show, Providence, RI.

David Delthony

"David Delthony," Gallery. *Woodwork Magazine*. April, 2006. p. 46-47.

"David Delthony." *Woodworker West Magazine*. Jan/Feb 2003, p. 54-55.

"David Delthony," http://artistsofutah.org/artists.

Ocvirk, Otto *et al. Art Fundamentals, Theory and Practice*. McGraw Hill Textbook for Higher Education, 11th edition, 2009, p. 44.

Don DeDobbeleer

"Don DeDobbeleer." *Woodworker West*. Mar-Apr 2008. pp. 54-55.

Skinner, Tina. *Studio Furniture, Today's Leading Woodworkers*. Schiffer Publishing Ltd. 2009

Doucette & Wolfe

Award

Juried into Early American Life 200 greatest craftsman in 2011 by *The Directory of Traditional American Crafts*. An artist who has been selected for the *Directory* has had his or her work thoroughly evaluated by a panel of experts. Because *Directory* artists so accurately replicate the styles and techniques of historic work, they might be mistaken for antiques. To assure this high-quality work is appreciated for the true quality of its modern craftsmanship, the *Directory* requires all work to be hallmarked.

David Ebner

Danto, Arthur. "Mutations of Function." *Craft Arts International*. 1995.

Perreault, John. "David Ebner. " *Explorations II*. The New Furniture American Craft Museum. 1991.

Heet, Erika. 1st Dibs - Creaters: David N. Ebner. 2010.

David Emery

Bogle, Michael, and Peta Landman. *Modern Australian Furniture*. Craftsman House. 1989.

Darby, Tom. *Making Fine Furniture*. Guild of Master Craftsman Publications. 1992.

"David Emery." *Australian Wood Review*. Spring/Summer 1992. pp. 8 -11.

Neil Erasmus

Contributing editor. *Australian Wood Review*. Quarterly (at least 15 to 20 articles over a 13-year period).

Glasgow, Andrew, and Ray Hemachandra. *500 Tables: Inspiring Interpretations of Function and Style*. New York and London: Lark Books, a Division of Sterling Publishing. 2009. p. 102.

Hemachandra, Ray, and John Grew Sheridan. *500 Cabinets: A Showcase of Design and Craftsmanship*. Asheville, NC: Lark Crafts. 2010.

Lloyd, Peter, and Andrew Crawford. *Celebrating Boxes*. Carmarthenshire, UK: Stobart Davies Ltd. 2001. pp. 60.

Scott Ernst

Caldwell, Brian. *Woodshop News*. Mar. 2005, pp 22-25

Pierce, Kerry. *The Custom Furniture Source Book: A Guide to 125 Craftsmen*. Newtown, CT: Taunton Press. 2001.

Sardy, Marin. *Santa Fe Magazine*. April/May 2010, pp 55

Brian Fireman

Goebel, Ann. "Fireman Finds His Footing." *Woodshop News*. January 2010: 33-35.

Glasgow, Andrew, and Ray Hemachandra. *500 Tables: Inspiring Interpretations of Function and Style*. New York and London: Lark Books, a Division of Sterling Publishing. 2009.

McLeroy, Merri Grace. "Brian Fireman – Woods of Art." *Broward Design*. Volume10/Number 5. 2009: 88-89.

Schafer, Romy. "Open-Shut." *Furniture Style*. September 2005: 106.

Mats Fogelvik

Glasgow, Andrew, and Ray Hemachandra. *500 Tables: Inspiring Interpretations of Function and Style*. New York and London: Lark Books, a Division of Sterling Publishing. 2009.

Hemachandra, Ray, and John Grew Sheridan. *500 Cabinets: A Showcase of Design and Craftsmanship*. Asheville, NC: Lark Crafts. 2010.

Pierce, Kerry. *The Custom Furniture Source Book: A Guide to 125 Craftsmen*. Newtown, CT: Taunton Press. 2001.

Shafto,Tiffany, DeEtte Shafto, and Lynda McDaniel. *Contemporary Hawaii Woodworkers*. Contemporary Publishers. 2009.

The HGTV show "Modern Masters" episode. MAS-911. 2004.

John Reed Fox

Dunnigan, John. et al. *The Heart of the Functional Arts*. The Furniture Society. 1999.

Harwood, Buie *et al. Architecture and Interior Design from the 19th Century to the Present: An Integrated History*. Harwood and May. 2005.

Lygate, Tony. *Award Winning Boxes*. New York: Sterling Publishing, 1995.

Lydgate, Tony. *The Art of Making Elegant Wood Boxes*. Sterling Publishing. 1992.

Pierce, Kerry. *The Custom Furniture Source Book*. Taunton Press. 2001.

PBS Woodwright's Shop." Japanese Planes with John Reed Fox." Season 26, Episode 8

Awards & Accolades

Niche Awards Finalist 2005.

Award of Excellence honorable mention, ACC Baltimore 2001.

Jason Frantz

Frantz, Jason, "Ode to a Doorknob." WoodShop Artisans Blog. May 2011.

Frantz, Jason, "Bloodwood Butterfly." WoodShop Artisans Blog Oct. 2010.

"From Corporate to Cabinet." *417 Home Magazine*. Fall 2006, pp. 20.

Ken and Julie Girardini

Coplan, Tina. "Craft Art at Home." *Home and Design Magazine*. Dec. 2007.

"Two of A Kind." BSO Show House. *Baltimore Sun*. May 2011.

Margery E. Goldberg

Hand, Larry. "Human Themes Important Theme for DC Sculptress." *Woodshop News*. Dec. 1988.

Lombardi, Lindsay. "I'm not the kind of girl… to be confined," *Northwest Passages*. May 21, 2008.

Magner, Jim. "Art & The City" *Hill Rag*. Sept. 2006.

Pelayo, Natalia. "Artist Spotlight" *Chevy Chase Patch*. Sept. 5, 2011.

Swift, Mary. "Sculptor, Art Entrepreneur, Curator, Zenith Gallery Owner/Director: Margery Goldberg" *Washington Review*, Aug/Sept 1993 p. 20.

Award

2010 Winner Mayors Arts Awards Washington DC

Tim Gorman

Abbey, Mary. "Review of Functional Sculpture." *Minneapolis Star-Tribune* Jan. 20, 2008. p. F-14.

"Functional Art Exhibition at Carleton." *Northfield News*. Jan. 5, 2008.

"Functional Sculpture: Furniture from the Upper Midwest" (online gallery), curated by Glenn Gordon and Laurel Bradley, Web: www.mnartists.org/tourHome.do?action=start&rid=173889

"Gallery: Northern Woods Exhibition 2005." *Woodwork #96*. Dec. 2005. p. 42.

"Gallery: Northern Woods Exhibition 2004." *Woodwork #90*. Dec. 2004. p. 52.

"Gallery: Timothy Gorman, Minneapolis, MN." *Woodwork*. #102. Dec. 2006, p. 44, 45.

Gordon, Glenn. "Functional Sculpture: An Eclectic Show of Furniture From the Upper Midwest." *Woodwork #112*. Aug. 2008, p. 59.

"Reader's Gallery." *Fine Woodworking #217*. Feb. 2011, p. 83.

"What Makes a House a Home?" (online gallery), curated by mnartists.org, http://mnartists.org/tourItemDetail.do?action=detail&rid=90615

Duncan Gowdy

"20 Minutes with Duncan Gowdy." *Furniture & Cabinetmaking Magazine*. June 2011. pp. 54-55.

"Carved in His Memory," *Fine Woodworking Magazine*. Dec. 2008. Cover.

Hemachandra, Ray, and John Grew Sheridan. *500 Cabinets: A Showcase of Design and Craftsmanship*. Asheville, NC: Lark Crafts. 2010.

"How They Did It: Man or Machine?" *Fine Woodworking Magazine*. Dec. 2008. pp. 108-109

Paul Gower

Norbury, Betty. *Furniture for the 21st Century*. Carmarthenshire, England: Stobart Davies Ltd. 1999.

Norbury, Betty. *Bespoke*. Carmarthenshire, England: Stobart Davies Ltd. 2007.

Glen G Guarino

Hemachandra, Ray. *500 Cabinets*. Ashland, NC: Lark Books. 2010.

Kapsales, Anissa. Producer Gina Eide. "Pro Portfolio." Fine Woodworking.com. 2008.

Richman, Alan. "An Artistic Approach." *Woodshop News*. Feb. 2009. pp. 35-37.

Skinner, Tina. *Studio Furniture from Today's Leading Woodworkers*. Atglen, PA: Schiffer Books. 2009.

Snyder, Jeffrey. *Wood Art Today 2*. Atglen, PA: Schiffer Books. 2010.

Jane Hall

Dickinson, Susan. "Color Outside the Borders. *Home Accent Today*. July 2011.

Peter Handler

Bolz, Diane. "The Timeless Art of Crafts." *Smithsonian*. May 2000.

Dormont, Linda. "Three Centuries of Philadelphia Furniture." *Art Matters*. April 1996.

Fisher, Marshall Jon. "The Ergonomic Rocking Chair." *Atlantic Monthly*. April 2001.

Forster, Laura. "Explosion of Color." *Daily Hampshire Gazette, Weekend Living*. Oct. 4-5, 1997.

Herman, Lloyd. "Art That Works: Decorative Arts of the Eighties, Crafted in America." Seattle, WA: University of Washington Press. 1989.

Furniture Studio. Books One and Two. The Furniture Society.

Harry Hare

Regular feature writer for *Furniture & Cabinet Making* magazine. GMC Publications Ltd., Lewes, East Sussex, UK. : Web: www.thegmcgroup.com

Peter Harrison

Binzen, Jon. "Material Dexterity." Focus on Materials: *Furniture Studio 4*, 2006. pp. 10-11.

Roger Heitzman

Glasgow, Andrew, and Hemachandra, Ray. *500 Tables: Inspiring Interpretations of Function and Style*. New York and London: Lark Books, a Division of Sterling Publishing. 2009.

Meilach, Dona Z. *Wood Art Today, Furniture, Vessels, Sculpture*. Atglen, PA: Schiffer Publishing. Sept. 2003.

Pierce, Kerry. *The Custom Furniture Source Book: A Guide to 125 Craftsmen*. Newtown, CT. Taunton Press. 2001.

Scotts Valley Patch. "The Path to Success is Carved From Wood." Dec 27, 2010, http://scottsvalley. patch.com/articles/the-path-to-success-is-carved-from-wood

"Square Peg in a Round Hole." *Fine Woodworking Magazine*. 2006 (#185).

"The Right Way to Use Contrast." Fine Woodworking. April 2010, http://Web: www.finewoodworking.com/item/24402/the-right-way-to-use-contrast.

"The Ultimate Layout and Assembly Table." *Woodwork*. June 2004.

Wood Works #9, Santa Cruz Community Television, April 2011 http://woodworks.blip.tv.

Awards & Accolades

Veneer Tech Craftsman Challenge. Honorable Mention (2 pieces), 2007.

Gail Rich Award. *Santa Cruz Sentinel*, Jan. 2004.

NW Fine Woodworking Box & Container Show. First Place, Seattle, WA, 2002.

Design in Wood, Third Place. San Diego County Fair, Del Mar, CA, 2002.

Jurors Award, Anything With A Drawer. Mesa Arts Center, Mesa, AZ, 2001.

Excellence in Craftsmanship Awards. *American Woodworker Magazine*, 1997, 1998.

Alfreda and Sam Maloof Scholarship. Anderson Ranch Art Center, Aspen, CO, 1990.

Jurors Award for Excellence. N. CA Woodworking Association, Mendocino, CA, 1982.

Alun Heslop

Boyer, Angie. "chaircreative." *Craft & Design*. Issue 195, Jan./Feb. 2008. p. 6-9.

Jones, Derek. "Furniture Classics." *Furniture & Cabinet Making*. Christmas 2009, Issue 161, p. 80.

Lloyd–Allum, Marc. "Sitting Pretty." *Luxure: The Cult of Luxury*. Sept. 201.

Savage, David. *Furniture with Soul: Master Woodworkers and Their Craft*. Tokyo, Japan: Kondansha International. 2011.

Mike Hindmarsh

Eichblatt, Sam. *Urbis Design*. Issue 57. pp. 110-111.

Forrester, Paul. *The Woodworkers Technique Bible*. New Burlington Press. 2009.

Tom Huang

"By Design." *Lawrence Journal World*. Feb. 25, 2007.

"Coolies – Weaving forms to celebrate connections and honor labor." *Review*. Mar. 2008.

"Furniture Makers show art can meet craft." *Philadelphia Inquirer*. May 7, 2010.

"Portfolio/Thomas Huang." *American Craft Magazine*. Dec./Jan. 2005/2006.

David Hubbard

Best of Worldwide Sculpture. Williamsburg, VA: Kennedy Publishing. 2011.

Hubbard, David. *The Shiny Shell*. Illustrated by Marcie Wolf-Hubbard. 2011.

Hubbard, David. "Glare," "Moments" and "Floaters." *Zouch Magazine*. Online literary magazine. 2011.

Slattery, Chris. "Art doctor: Hubbard creates, curates and installs," *Gazette Newspaper*. June 20, 2007. http://ww2.gazette.net/stories/062007/entenew230857_32373.shtml.

Millstone, Ken. "Potomac Elementary Sculpts Artistic Future, David Hubbard's "Night Boat" is among first public artworks in Potomac," The Almanac. Nov. 10, 2005. http://Web: www.connectionnewspapers.com/article.asp?article=251620&paper=70&cat=104.

Derek Hurd

"Anjali Athavaley." *Wall Street Journal*. April 20, 2011. A Little Something Different. Life & Culture. p.1.

"Audrey Dutton." *Idaho Statesman Business Insider*. May 18th, 2011. Page 3.

Rachel Hutchinson

Norbury, Betty. *Bespoke: Source Book of Furniture Designer Makers*. Carmarthenshire, UK: Stobart Davies. 2009.

Norbury, Betty. *Furniture for the 21st Century*. Carmarthenshire, UK: 1999.

Norbury, Betty. *British Craftsmanship in Wood*. Carmarthenshire, UK: 1990.

Silas Kopf

Kopf, Silas. *A Marquetry Odyssey*. Manchester, VT: Hudson Hills Press. 2008.

Nicholas Langan

"Journeyman Furniture." *Craft and Design Magazine*. July/Aug. 2011. pp. 72-73.

"A Journeyman's Tale." *Cornwall Life Magazine*. Sept. 2009. pp. 70-71.

Dave LeBleu

LeBleu, Dave. "Adirondack Furniture." Eastern Mass Guild of Woodworkers (EMGW). 2005.

LeBleu, Dave. "Why I wear Eye Protection." Eastern Mass Guild of Woodworkers (EMGW), Sept. 2009 and reprinted Web: www.eliotschool.org/nod.

Paul Malmendier

"Artisan Paul Malmendier, Metalsmith." *Home Magazine*. April 2005.

"Man of Steel." *Philadelphia Magazine Home & Garden, Fall/Winter*. 2004. pp. 114-117, 151-154.

HGTV's Modern Masters. Aug. 2003.

Alison J. McLennan

Hemachandra, Ray, and John Grew Sheridan. *500 Cabinets: A Showcase of Design and Craftsmanship*. Asheville, NC: Lark Crafts. 2010.

Glasgow, Andrew, and Ray Hemachandra. *500 Tables: Inspiring Interpretations of Function and Style*. New York and London: Lark Books, a Division of Sterling Publishing. 2009.

Kelsey, John. *Furniture Studio 3: Furniture Makers Exploring Digital Technologies*. Asheville, NC: The Furniture Society. 2005.

Hansson, Bobby. *The Fine Art of the Tin Can: Techniques and Inspirations*. Asheville, NC: Lark Books. 2005.

"Show Us Your Drawers." *Exhibition catalog*. Indianapolis, IN: The Herron Gallery, Herron School of Art, Indiana University/Purdue University, Indianapolis. 2006.

Carlos Motta

Fialdini, Romulo et al. *Carlos Motta*. São Paulo: DBA Artes Gráficas, 2004. Translation to English Thomas Nerney.

Motta, Carlos Lichtenfels. *Carlos Motta: life as I see it*. São Paulo: Bei Comunicação, 2010.

Bienal Ibero-Americana de Design Bid_08 (Catalog) Coordinación Y edición: EQUIPO BID-DIMAD Gráfica Muriel, 2008.

Bienal Brasileira de Design (3: 2010: Curitiba, PR) – Catalog

III Bienal Brasileira de Design / Main / Head Curator Adélia Borges; (English translation Traduzca. com). – 1. Ed. – Curitiba, PR: Centro de Design do Paraná, 2010

Jeff O'Brien

Gibson, Scott (Ed.). *Fine Woodworking Design: Original Furniture from the World's Finest Craftsmen*, aka Design Book Eight. Newtown, CT: Taunton Press. Mar. 1, 2009.

Hemachandra, Ray, and John Grew Sheridan, authors. *500 Cabinets: A Showcase of Design and Craftsmanship*. Asheville, NC: Lark Crafts. 2010.

Berto Pandolfo

Fischer, Joachim, *Young Asian Designers* DAAB. (Germany). 2005. pp. 252-255.

McEoin, E. and V. Stappmans. *The Sydney Design Guide*. Australia: Alphabet Press. 2008/09. p. 97.

Stening, Belinda. "A Pragmatic Italian." *Curve* (Australia) Issue 11, 2005. pp. 20-24.

Timothy Philbrick

"Classic Proportions." *Fine Woodworking Magazine*. Winter 1977. cover & pp. 39-43.

Cooke, Edward. *New American Furniture*. Boston Museum of Fine Arts. 1989.

Cooke, Edward et al. *The Makers Hand*. Boston Museum of Fine Arts. 2003.

"Designing with Dividers." *Home Furniture Magazine*. Summer 1996. pp. 84-89.

Fitzgerald, Oscar. *Studio Furniture of the Renwick Gallery*. Fox Chapel. 2007.

Ramljak, Suzanne. *Crafting a Legacy*. Contemporary Crafts in The Philadelphia Museum of Art. 2002.

Andrew Pitts

"His New Call to Duty." *Woodshop News*. April 2010. pp. 46-49.

Skinner, Tina. *Studio Furniture, Today's Leading Woodworkers*. Atglen, PA: Schiffer Publishing, June 2010.

VanderHoeven, Nakisha. *Fine Wood Artists*. Blurb, Inc.

Charles Ramberg

Charleston Post & Courier. Oct 14, 2002. & May 7, 2000.

Charleston Style & Design. Summer 2009.

House Beautiful. Fall 2009 & July 2003. Cover.

David Rasmussen

"Form and Function." *Aspen Sojourner*. Midsummer 2011. pp. 75.

"The High Life." *Colorado Homes and Lifestyles*. June/July 2011. pp. 44-49.

"Style Maker." *Luxe*. Spring 2011. pp. 132-133.

"Profile: David Rasmussen." *Woodworker West*. Nov./Dec. 2010. pp. 54-55.

"Built to Last." *Aspen Sojourner*. Midsummer 2010. pp. 36.

Jodi Robbins

Fenton, Cheryl. "William Henry's New Home." *Stuff Magazine*. Nov. 2010.

Award

Best of Boston Home. Winner 2009.

Kevin Rodel

Blankemeyer, Dennis. *Crafts Furniture; Legacy of the Human Hand*. Atglen, PA: Schiffer Publishers. 2003.

Dunnigan John, et al. *Furniture Studio; The Heart of the Functional Arts*. Free Union, VA: The Furniture Society. 1999.

Hemachandra, Ray, and John Grew Sheridan, authors. *500 Cabinets: A Showcase of Design and Craftsmanship*. Asheville, NC: Lark Crafts. 2010.

Rodel, Kevin, and Jonathan Binzen. *Arts & Crafts Furniture; from Classic to Contemporary*. Newtown, CT; Taunton Press, 2003.

Rodel, Kevin. "A Study in Squares." *Fine Woodworking Magazine*. Aug. 2011. pp. 60-67.

Smith, Bruce, and Yoshiko Yamamoto. *The Beautiful Necessity*. Layton, Utah: Gibbs Smith Publishers. 1996.

Jo Roessler

Arts and Crafts Home and the Revival – Bed by Name, Summer 2010. pp. 19.

Arts and Crafts Home and the Revival – Rosewood In Relief, Summer 2010, pp. 38.

Blankemeyer, Dennis. *Craft Furniture: The Legacy of the Human Hand*. Atglen, PA: Schiffer Publishing. June 2003.

Fine Woodworking: Design Book 7: 360 Photographs of the Best Work in Wood: Newtown, CT: Taunton Press. Sept. 1996.

Harryet Candee. "The Artful Mind – Jo Roessler, Nojo Design," *Furniture Maker*, Aug. 2010, pp. 12-14.

Home and Garden Television – "Modern Masters." MAS-705.

Meilach, Dona Z. *Wood Art Today, Furniture, Vessels, Sculpture*. Atglen, PA: Schiffer Publishing. Sept. 2003.

Pierce, Kerry. *The Custom Furniture Source Book: A Guide to 125 Craftsmen*. Newtown, CT: Taunton Press. 2001.

Snyder, Jeffrey B., Ed., *Wood Art Today 2*. Atglen, PA: Schiffer Publishing, June 2010.

"Tom Vannah." *Preview Magazine – Mr. Majestic*, Spring 2006. pp. 31-34.

WGBY. "Paradise City Fall 2004 Collection," Oct. 2004.

Woodworking… In Action: Gallery "Machine Processes – A Pair of Small Doors." Issue 10. Jan. 2008.

Sylvie Rosenthal

"Emerging Artist." *American Style Magazine*. Aug. 2009. p. 55.

Glasgow, Andrew, and Ray Hemachandra. *500 Tables: Inspiring Interpretations of Function and Style*. New York and London: Lark Books, a Division of Sterling Publishing. 2009.

Glasgow, Andrew. "Juxtapositions." *American Craft Magazine*. Feb/Mar. 2010. pp. 24-25.

Hemachandra, Ray. *500 Chairs: Celebrating Traditional and Innovative Designs*. New York and London: Lark Books, a Division of Sterling Publishing. 2008.

Alex Roskin

Fine Woodworking Design Book Seven. 1996
Passport, Summer 2005
Rhode Island Business Journal, April 1999

Alfred Sharp

Skinner, Tina. *Studio Furniture, Today's Leading Woodworkers*. Atglen, PA: Schiffer Publishing, June 2010.

Joel Shepard

"Mastering the Art of Furniture." *Architectural Digest*. Oct. 2005.

"Antique-look, modern function." *Architectural Record*.

Fuad-Luke, Alastair. *eco Design, The Sourcebook*. San Francisco, CA: Chronicle Books. 2002. pp. 47, 310.

"Living with nature." *Luxe Interiors + Design*.

Prinzing, Debra. "Regions top interior designers reveal trends." *The Seattle Times*. Feb 27, 2005.

Perspectives on Design- Pacific Northwest. Plano, TX: Panache Partners 2010.

Stender, W. Thomas, ed. *The Penland Book of Woodworking: Masterclasses in Woodworking Techniques*. The "Gallery" section of the chapter by Martin Puryear. New York, NY: Lark Books. 2007. p. 66.

Tolpin, Jim. *Built-in Furniture*. Newtown, CT: Taunton Press. 1997. pp. 72-73,117-118.

Kelsey, John, and Rick Mastelli, eds. *Furniture Studio: the Heart of the Functional Arts*. In the article "From a Distance by Roger Holmes." Free Union, VA: The Furniture Society. 1999. p. 63.

Rich Soborowicz

Dresdner, Michael. "Simplicity via Subtle Complexity." *Woodworkers Journal*. Issue 225 June 2009.

Hemachandra, Ray, and John Grew Sheridan. *500 Cabinets: A Showcase of Design and Craftsmanship*. Asheville, NC: Lark Crafts. 2010.

Robert Spangler

Caldwell, Brian. "Concentrated Effort." *Woodshop News*. April 2002. pp. 28-30.

Fine Woodworking. *Design Book Six*. Nagyszalancy, Sandor, ed. Newtown, CT: The Taunton Press Inc. 199.

Hemachandra, Ray, and Craig Nutt. *500 Chairs: Celebrating Traditional & Innovative Design*. Ashland, NC: Lark Books. 2008.

Hemachandra, Ray. *Lark Book Series: Chairs*. Ashland, NC: Lark Books. 2010.

Spangler, Robert. "Community Effort Shines After 30 Years." *Woodshop News*. Jan. 2011. pp. 22-23.

Teague, Matthew. "Six Ways to Build a Bed." *Fine Woodworking Magazine*. Aug. 2011. pp. 30-37.

The Furniture Society. *The Heart of the Functional Arts*. Kelsey, John, & Rick Mastelli, eds. Bethel, CT: Cambium Press, 1999.

Nick Strange

Fisher, Thomas. *Progressive Architecture*. Feb. 1995. pp. 72–77.

Laurence, Vincent. *Fine Woodworking*. April 1992. pp. 72.

Mays, Vernon. *Inform*. 1997. Number two. pp. 14–17.

Strange, Meredith, and Nick Strange. "Working With Artisans For Greener Places of Worship." *Faith and Form*. 2008. Vol. XLI. pp. 12–15.

Larion Swartzendruber

Lehman, Bruce. "Wright At Home In Lake Setting." *Northern Indiana Lakes Magazine*. 2006. pp. 66 - 69.

Lind, Carla. *Wright Style: Re-Creating the Spirit of Frank Lloyd Wright*. New York, NY: Simon & Schuster. 1992. pp. 192, 193, 194.

Saoud, Angela. "Quality, Details in Swartzendruber Designs." *Northern Indiana Lakes Magazine*. Sept. /Oct. 2006. p. 21.

Skolnik, Lisa. *Prairie Style*. Sterling Publishing. 2006. pp. 15, 80, 81, 83.

Craig Thibodeau

"Exotic Inlays by Craig Thibodeau." *Fine Woodworking Magazine*. Jan-Feb 2011. pp. 90-93.

"For the Love of Furniture." *Romantic Homes Magazine*. Sept. 2009. pp 19-20.

Gibson, Scott, and Peter Turner. *Blanket Chests: Outstanding Designs from 30 of the World's Finest Furniture Makers*. Newtown, CT: Taunton Press. 2011.

Skinner, Tina. *Studio Furniture, Today's Leading Woodworkers*. Atglen, PA: Schiffer Publishing Ltd. 2009

Thomas Throop

Hemachandra, Ray, and John Grew Sheridan. *500 Cabinets: A Showcase of Design and Craftsmanship*. Asheville, NC: Lark Crafts. 2010.

Home Furniture Magazine. Article and Cover. Newton, CT: Taunton Press. Spring 1996.

Meilach, Dona Z. *Wood Art Today, Furniture, Vessels, Sculpture*. Atglen, PA: Schiffer Publishing. Sept. 2003.

Snyder, Jeff. *Wood Art Today 2*. Atglen, PA: Schiffer Publishing, 2010.

Pierce, Kerry. *The Custom Furniture Source Book: A Guide to 125 Craftsmen*. Newtown, CT: Taunton Press. 2001.

Doug Turner

http://Web: www.finewoodworking.com/item/31928/a-conversation-with-professional-woodworker-doug-turner

http://Web: www.finewoodworking.com/item/34732/communicating-with-clients

http://Web: www.finewoodworking.com/item/31142/seek-first-not-to-offend

http://Web: www.inewoodworking.com/item/35189/odd-projects-and-odder-clients-tips-on-best-practices

http://Web: www.finewoodworking.com/item/35482/bartering-for-free-advertising

http://Web: www.finewoodworking.com/item/35611/a-paradigm-shift-part-1

http://Web: www.finewoodworking.com/item/35733/a-paradigm-shift-part-2

http://Web: www.finewoodworking.com/item/35851/a-paradigm-shift-final-installment

Peter S. Turner

"25th Anniversary Issue." *Fine Woodworking*. Winter 2000/2001.

Gibson, Scott, and Peter Turner. *Blanket Chests: Outstanding Designs from 30 of the World's Finest Furniture Makers*. Newtown, CT: Taunton Press. 2011.

Gibson, Scott. *Design Book Eight*. Newton, CT: Taunton Press. 2009. p. 120.

"Hickory and Ash Blanket Chest." *Fine Woodworking*. Feb. 2009. pp. 54 – 61.

"Peter Turner: Profile." *Woodwork*. Winter 2011.

Pierce, Kerry. *The Custom Furniture Source Book*. Newton, CT: The Taunton Press. 2001.

Fredrick C. Vogt

"A Conservation Collaborative: The James Monroe gilded ceremonial armchair." *The Magazine Antiques*. Mar. 2010. pp. 78 - 83.

"Conservation of a Boulle Marquetry Bracket Clock." *Antiques and Fine Art Magazine*. Summer/Autumn 2006. pp. 185 –188.

"Preserving History." *Furniture and Interiors Magazine*. Summer 2004.

"Vetting the Winter Antique Show." *Antiques and Fine Art Magazine*. 6th Anniversary. Issue 2005. p. 42.

Seth Walter

Furniture and Cabinetmaking Magazine, Maker's Gallery featured maker. Jan. 2009. p. 29.

Furniture and Cabinetmaking Magazine. Reader's Gallery award winner. Sept. 2007. p. 74.

Private Varnish Magazine. Oct. 2008. pp. 28-31.

South Windsor Life Magazine. Artist profile, cover page. Jan. 2011. pp. 43-45.

Woodwork Magazine. Dec. 2007. p. 44.

Peter Wehrspann

Laws, A. "Room To View." Retrieved Aug. 20, 2011. From http://Web: www.eyeweekly.com/style/myplace/article/18594.

Magarrey, P. "Interior Visions." Retrieved Aug. 20, 2011. From http://Web: www.azuremagazine.com/newsviews/blog_content.php?id=820.

Modern Karibou. "Interview With Peter Wehrspann." Retrieved Aug. 20, 2011, from http://blog.modernkaribou.ca/2009/06/youve-indicated-that-you-love-working-on-custom-pieces-whats-your-dream-commission--i-believe-i-have-had-a-couple-dre.html.

Wehrspann, P. "We The Consumed Exhibition Website." Retrieved Aug. 20, 2011. From http://Web: www.wetheconsumed.com/contact.html.

Rex D. White

Fine Woodworking Design Book Three. Newtown, CT: Taunton Press. 1983. p. 92.

"Good Save." *Metropolitan Home Magazine*. Mar./April 2003. pp. 100-107.

"Studio Hopping in Fredericksburg," *Texas Highways Magazine*. Jan. 2004. pp. 56-57.

"Tradition with a Twist." *Timber Home Living Magazine*. June 2011. p. 16.

Mark Whitley

"Mark Whitley – WoodCraftsman." *Arts Across Kentucky*. Summer 2007, pp.13-16.

Stamps, Kathie. "Functional Art." *Kentucky Homes and Gardens*. May-June 2011. pp. 30-33.

Woodwork back cover feature, winter 2011. pp. 13-16.

John Wesley Williams

Schenk, Joseph B. *Celebrating the Creative Spirit. Contemporary Southeast Furniture*. Mobile Museum press. 1998.

Erik Wolken

Guild Artists. *Object Lessons: Beauty and Meaning in Art*. Madison, WI: Guild Publishing. 2001.

Kelsey, John. *Furniture Studio: Furniture Makers Exploring Digital Technologies*. Asheville, NC: The Furniture Society. 2005.

Portfolio section. *American Craft Magazine*. Jan. 2002.

Skinner, Tina. *Studio Furniture, Today's Leading Woodworkers*. Atglen, PA: Schiffer Publishing Ltd. 2009.

Edward Wohl

Caldwell, Brian. "Chairman of the Boards." *Woodshop News*. Dec. 2002. pp. T31-T33.

Hemachandra, Ray, ed. *500 Cabinets: A Showcase of Design & Craftsmanship*. New York, NY: Lark Books. 2010.

Kelsey, John, ed. *Furniture Makers Exploring Digital Technologies*. Bethel, CT: Cambium Press. 2005.

Smith, Paul J., ed. *Objects for Use | Handmade by Design*. New York, NY: Harry N Abrams, Inc. 2001.

Leah Woods

"Content That Works." *Wood, Revisited*. Issue 5. 2007.

"Emerging Artists." *American Style Magazine*. Feb. 2007.

Hemachandra, Ray, ed. *500 Cabinets: A Showcase of Design & Craftsmanship*. New York, NY: Lark Books. 2010.

Fine Woodworking Design Book Eight. Newtown, CT: Taunton Press.

Fine Woodworking Furniture: 102 Contemporary Designs. Newtown, CT: Taunton Press. 2008.

Hemachandra, Ray and Craig Nutt. *500 Chairs: Celebrating Traditional & Innovative Design*. Ashland, NC: Lark Books. 2008.

Yoko Zeltserman-Miyaji

Oka, Midori. "The Indulgence of Design in Japanese Art." *Arts of Asia*. Vol. 36, no. 3. 2006.

Where Their Work Is Found

William Acland
Web: www.Watersandacland.co.uk
Shown at:
• Liberty London, London, UK W1B5AH
• Waters & Acland, Staveley, Nr Kendal, Cumbria, UK LA8 9LR

Bruce Bartholomew
Web: www.bgbartholomew.com
Web: www.berkshirewoodworkers.org

Brian Benhan
Web: www.benhamdesignconcepts.com

Robert Brou
Web: www. naturalismfurniture.com
Shown at:
• Naturalism Furniture, Atlanta, GA 30307

Guy Bucchi
Web: www.guybucchi.com

Tom Calhoun
Web: www.worldwoodworks.com
Shown at:
• Dennis Holzer Gallery, Makawao, HI 96768
• Hana Coast Gallery, Hana, HI, 96713
• Na Pua Gallery, Kihei, HI 96753

Tim Coleman
Web: www.timothycoleman.com
Shown at:
• Dane Gallery, Nantucket, MA 02554
• New Hampshire Furniture Masters, Manchester, NH 03108
• Pritam and Eames, East Hampton, NY 11937
• William Zimmer Gallery, Mendocino, CA 95460

Stephen Courtney
Web: www.stephencourtney.com

Ed Cruikshank
Web: www.cruikshank.co.nz
Shown at:
• Cruikshank Ltd., Arrowtown 9302, Central Otago, NZ

Michael Daniel
Web: www.michaeldanielmetal.com

Don DeDobbeleer
Web: www.finecustomwoodfurniture.com
Shown at:
• Gallery M, Half Moon Bay, CA 94019
• Inscapes Gallery, Newport, OR 97365

Randy DeGraw
Web: www.viewwoodwork.com.au
Web: www.randydegraw.com
Email: randydegraw@gmail.com
Shown at:
• Randy DeGraw Studio Gallery, Maleny, Queensland, Australia

Mark Del Guidice
Web: www.markdelguidice.com
Shown at:
• Mark Del Guidice Furniture, Norwood, MA 02062
• CraftBoston, World Trade Center & Cyclorama, Boston, MA
• Gallery Naga 02116, Boston, MA 02116
• Philadelphia Museum of Art Craft Show, Philadelphia, PA
• Smithsonian Craft Show, Washington, DC
• Society of Arts and Crafts, Boston, MA 02116

Joe della-Porta
Web: www.della-porta.co.uk
Shown at:
• Langton Green Gallery, UK TN3 0HP

David Delthony
Web: www.SculpturedFurnitureArtandCeramics.com
Shown at:
• Sculptured Furniture, Art & Ceramics, Escalante, UT 84726

Moriah Doucette and Matthew Wolfe
Web: www.doucetteandwolfefurniture.com
Shown at:
• Doucette and Wolfe Furniture Makers, Center Conway, NH 03813

David Ebner
Web: www.davidneber.com
Shown at:
• Moderne Gallery, Philadelphia, PA 19106
• Pritam & Eames, East Hampton, New York 11937
• SOFA, Web: www.sofaexpo.com

David Emery
Web:
www.davidemery-furnituremaker.com.au
Shown at:
• Bungendore Wood Works Gallery, Bungendore NSW, Australia
• Image Interiors, Richmond Victoria, Australia

Neil Erasmus
Web: www.erasmusdesigns.com
Email: erasmus@erasmusdesigns.com
Shown at:
• Erasmus Designs, Pickering Brook, Western Australia 6076
• Bungendore Woodworks Gallery, Bungendore, New South Wales, Australia 2621

Scott Ernst
Web: www. ScottErnstFurniture.com
Shown at:
• La Mesa of Santa Fe, Santa Fe, NM 87501
• Made in the Shade, Santa Fe NM 87501

S. D. Feather
Web: www.custommade.com/by/sd-feather/ projects/
Shown at:
• Lehigh Valley Builders Show, Bethlehem, PA
• NeoCon East, Baltimore, MD 21201
• The Philadelphia Furniture Show, Philadelphia, PA

Brian Fireman
Web: www.brianfiremandesign.com
Email: bfireman@brianfiremandesign.com
Shown at:
• August Avery, Atlanta, GA 30305
• BON, balance order nature, Miami, FL 33145
• DESIGNLUSH, New York, NY 10016
• Elan Collections, Las Vegas, NV 89118
• Siglo Moderno, Los Angeles, CA 90069

Mats Fogelvik
Web: www.fogelvik.com
mats@fogelvik.com
Shown at:
• Cliff Johns Gallery, Holualoa, HI 96725
• Hana Coast Gallery, Hana, HI 96713
• Isaacs Art Center, Kamuela, HI
• Volcano Art Center, Volcano, HI 96785

John Reed Fox
Web: www: johnreedfox.com

Jason Frantz
Web: www.woodshopartisans.com
Shown at:
WoodShop Artisans (by appointment)
Springfield, MO 65804

Reagan Furqueron
Web: www.reaganfurqueron.com

Ken and Julie Girardini
Web: www.girardinidesign.com
Web: www.giradinifineart.com
Web: www.artfulhome.com
Shown at:
• Gallery Five, Tequesta, FL 33469
• Mimosa Gallery, Saratoga Springs, NY 12866
• SweetHeart Gallery, Woodstock NY 12498
• Zenith Gallery, Chevy Chase, MD 20015

Margery E. Goldberg
Web: www.zenithgallery.com
Margery@zenithgallery.com
Shown at:
• Zenith Gallery, Inc., Washington DC 20015

Tim Gorman
Web: www.gormanartanddesign.com
Web: www.mnartists.org/artistHome.do?rid=22851
Web: www.mnwwg.org

Duncan Gowdy
Web: www: duncangowdy.com
Shown at:
• MB Stahl Interiors, West Newton, MA 02465
• Pritam & Eames, East Hampton, NY 11937

Paul Gower
Web: www.paulgowerfurniture.co.uk

Glen G Guarino
Web: www.guarinofurnituredesigns.com
Shown at:
• BeSpoke Global, New York, NY 10016

Tracy Gumm
Email: tracy@irminsul.com.au

Jane Hall
Web: www.janehalldesign.com
Web: www.custommade.com/by/janehalldesign
Web: www.behance.net/janehall design
Shown at:
• Jane Hall - The Voice of Style, Toronto ON CA M4M2E1

Peter Handler
Web: www.handlerstudio.com
Shown at:
• Grovewood Gallery, Asheville, NC 28804
• Handler Studio, Philadelphia, PA 19129
• Zenith Gallery, Washington, DC 20012

Harry Hare
Web: www.harryhare.co.uk

Peter Harrison
Web: www.lavassa.com

John and Andrea Hartcorn
Web: www.hartcorndesign.com
Shown at:
• Home Portfolio.com
• ACC Baltimore crafts show

Roger Heitzman
Web: www.heitzmanstudios.com
Shown at:
• Act One Gallery, Taos, NM 87571
• Gallery M, Half Moon Bay, CA 94019
• Garden Accents, West Conshohocken, PA 19428
• Garden Artisans, Annapolis, MD 21401
• Great Place, Carmel, CA 93923
• VUE Gallery, Sedona, AZ 86336

John Herbert
Shown at:
• Banks Gallery, Portsmouth, NH 03801
• Shaw Cramer Gallery, Vineyard Haven, MA 02568
• WallWork Gallery, Rockport, ME 04856

Alun Heslop
Web: www.chaircreative.com
Email: alun@chaircreative.com
Shown at:
• The Workshop, Sussex, England (by appointment)

Mike Hindmarsh
Web: www.mikehindmarsh.com

Tom Huang
Web: www.TomHuangStudio.com
Web: www.bamboocanoe.biz
Shown at:
• Shidoni Gallery, Tesuque NM 87574
• Wexler Gallery, Philadelphia, PA 19106
• William Zimmer Gallery, Mendocino, CA 95460

David Hubbard
Web: www.hubbardsfinenearts.com

Derek Hurd
Web: www.studio12-12.com
Email: derek@studio12-12.com

Rachel Hutchinson
Web: www.rachelhutchinson.co.uk
Web: www.photostore.org.uk
Web: www.furnituremkrs.co.uk
Web: www.makerseye.co.uk
Shown at:
• Gallery, Contemporary Applied Arts, London, W1T 1DD

Derrick Ibbott
Web: www.derrickibbott.co.uk

Gary Inman
Web: www.GARYINMAN.com

Rick Jasinski
Web: www.JasinskiFurniture.com
Web: www.craftsmanwoodshop.com

Robert Kernohan
Email: info@kernohan.co.uk
Shown at:
• Robert Kernohan Furniture, Antrim, N Ireland (by appointment)

David Kirkland
Web: www.davidkirklandcabinetmaker.co.nz

Silas Kopf
Web: www.silaskopf.com

Nicholas Langan
Web: www.journeymanfurniture.co.uk
Shown at:
- Cornwall Crafts, Trelowarren Gallery, Cornwall UK
- Cornwall Crafts, Trelissick Gallery, Cornwall UK
- Journeyman Furniture Studio and Gallery, Hayle, Cornwall. UK

Dave LeBleu
Web: www.LeBleuFurniture.com

George Mahoney
george@solvstudio.com
Email: george_mahoney@mcad.edu

Paul Malmendier
Web: www.artmetalworks.com

Harv Mastalir
Web: www.harvmastalir.com

Alison J. McLennan
Web: www.ajm-furniture.com
Shown at:
- Gallery NAGA, Boston, MA 02116
- Mobilia Gallery, Cambridge, MA 02138
- Stewart Kummer Gallery, Gualala, CA 95445

Carlos Motta
Web: www.carlosmotta.com.br
Shown at:
- Atelier Carlos Motta, São Paulo, Brazil
- Espasso Inc. New York, New York, USA
- Espasso Inc. Gallery LA, Los Angeles, USA

Jeff O'Brien
Web: www.dogwood-design.com
Shown at:
- Dogwood Design, West Linn, OR 97068

Berto Pandolfo
Web: www.bertopandolfo.com
Shown at:
- Chee Soon and Fitzgerald, Sydney, Australia
- Tongue and Groove, Melbourne, Victoria, Australia

Timothy Philbrick
Web: www.timothyphilbrick.com
Shown at:
- Gallery NAGA, Boston, MA 02116
- Pritem & Eames, East Hampton, NY 11937

Henry Pilcher
Web: www.henrypilcher.com
Shown at:
- Anibou, Redfern NSW 2016

Andrew Pitts
Web: www.AndrewPittsFurnitureMaker.com
Web: www.ArtfulHome.com
Web: www.FineWoodArtists.com
Shown at:
- Studio Gallery, Kilmarnock, VA 22482
- The Artisans Center, Virginia Gallery at the Artisphere, Arlington, VA 22209

Charles Ramberg
Web: www.rambergfurniture.com

Amanda Ransom
Web: www.englishfurnitureworkshop.co.uk
Shown at:
- Burford Garden Company, Burford, Oxfordshire, England, OX18 4PA
- Liberty of London, London, England W1B 5AH

David Rasmussen
Web: www.davidrasmussendesign.com
Web: www.custommade.com/by/davidrasmussen
Shown at:
- Anderson Art Ranch, Snowmass Village, CO 81615
- North West Fine Woodworking Gallery, Seattle, Washington 98104

David Michael Redwine
Web: www.redwinefurniture.com
Email: david@redwinefurniture.com

Jodi Robbins
Web: www.williamhenryfurniture.com
Shown at:
- Half Crown Design & William Henry Furniture, Cambridge MA 02138

Kevin Rodel
Web: www.kevinrodel.com
Shown at:
- Messler Gallery, Rockport, ME 04011

Jo Ruskin Roessler
Web: www.NojoDesign.com
Email: info@nojodesign.com

Sylvie Rosenthal
Web: www.sylvierosenthal.com
Email: info@sylvierosenthal.com
Shown at:
- del Mano Gallery, Los Angeles, CA 90025
- Penland Gallery, Penland, NC 28765
- Signature Shop, Atlanta, GA 30305

Alex Roskin
Web: www. alexroskin.com
Shown at:
- Phillips De Pury, New York, NY 10022
- Sharada Gallery, Hudson NY 12534
- Wexler Gallery, Philadelphia, PA 19106

Joram Schurmans
Web: www.ramfurniture.be
Email: info@ramfurniture.be

Alfred Sharp
Web: www.alfredsharp.com

Joel Shepard
Web: www.joelshepardfurniture.com.

Jules Siegel
Shown at:
Lexington Arts and Crafts Society
Lexington, MA 02421

Janice Claire Smith
Web: www.janicesmithfurniture.com
Email: not2wooden@earthlink.net

Rich Soborowicz
Web: www.finewoodstudio.com
Shown at:
- Northwest Fine Woodworking, 101 S. Jackson St., Seattle, WA 98104
- Real Mother Goose, 901 SW Yamhill Street, Portland, OR 97205

Robert Spangler
Web: www.rspangler.com
Shown at:
- NW Fine Woodworking, Seattle, WA 98104
- Robert Spangler Studio, Bainbridge Island, WA 98110 (by appointment)
- The Island Gallery, Bainbridge Island, WA 98110
- The Real Mother Goose, Portland, OR 97205

Lex Stobie
Web: www.lexstobiedesign.com
Shown at:
- Great Dane Furniture, Melbourne, Sydney, and Brisbane, Australia
- Tongue and Groove, Melbourne, Victoria, Australia

Nick Strange
Web: www.thecenturyguild.com
Web: www.anthonyclaret.com
Shown at:
- The Century Guild, Ltd., Carrboro, NC 27510

Larion Swartzendruber
Web: www.swartzendruber.com
Email: larion@swartzendruber.com
Shown at:
- Swartzendruber Furniture Creations, Goshen, Indiana 46528

Craig Thibodeau
Web: www.ctfinefurniture.com
Shown at:
- Dovetail Collection, Healdsburg, CA 95448

Thomas Throop
Web: www.blackcreekdesigns.com
Shown at:
- Silvermine Arts Guild, New Canaan, CT 06840

Kent Townsend
Web: www.kenttownsend.com
Shown at:
- Jane Sauer Gallery, Sante Fe, NM 87501

Doug Turner
Web: www.TurnerCustomFurniture.com
Email: Doug@TurnerCustomFurniture.com
Shown at:
- Turner Custom Furniture, Atlanta, GA 30339

Peter S. Turner
Web: www.petersturner.com
Shown at:
- The Gallery at Frenchman's Bay, Ellsworth, ME 04605
- Thos. Moser Showroom, Freeport, ME 04032
- Trinket and Fern, Portland, ME 04101

Fredrick C. Vogt
Web: www.vogtconservation.com
Shown at:
- F.C. Vogt Company, Inc., Richmond, VA 23220

Seth Walter
Web: www.silverleafwoodworking.com

Peter Wehrspann
Web: www.holtzundmetal.com
Shown at:
- Haliburton Sculpture Forest, Haliburton, ON, CA
- Modern Karibou, Ottawa, ON, CA
- Verso Furniture Inc., Shelburne, ON, CA

Lewis Wexler
Web: wexlergallery.com

Rex D. White
Web: www.rexwhitecustomfurniture.com
Shown at:
- RS Hanna Gallery, Fredericksburg, TX 78624

Mark Whitley
Web: www.mwhitley.com
Shown at:
- The Grovewood Gallery, Asheville, NC 28804
- Salvo Collective, Louisville, KY 40402
- Kentucky Museum of Art and Craft, Louisville, KY 40202
- The Kentucky Artisan Center, Berea, KY 40403

John Wesley Williams
Web: www.johnwesleywilliamsfurniture.com
Web: www.Artfulhome.com
Shown at:
- Bennetts Gallery, Knoxville, TN 37919
- Creations Gallery, Hockessin, DE 19707
- Grovewood Gallery, Ashville, NC 28804
- Piedmont Craftsmen, Winston Salem, NC 27101
- Southern Highland Craft Guild, Ashville, NC 28805
- Tamarack-Best of West Virginia, Beckley, WV 25801
- Washington Street Gallery, Lewisburg, WV 24901
- WV Living Gallery, Snowshoe, WV 26291

Edward Wohl
Web: www.edwardwohl.com

Erik Wolken
Web: www.erikwolken.com
Web: www.custommade.com
Web: www.finewoodartists.com
Shown at:
- Society for Contemporary Craft, Pittsburgh, PA 15222

Leah Woods
Web: www.leahkwoods.com
Shown at
- The Center for Art in Wood, Philadelphia, PA 19106
- New Hampshire Furniture Masters Association, Manchester, NH 03108

Nico Yektai
Web: www.nicoyektai.com
Shown at:
- LongHouse Reserve, East Hampton, NY 11937

Yoko Zeltserman-Miyaji
Web: www.yokomiyaji.com
Shown at:
- Mobilia Gallery, Cambridge, MA 02138

Galleries & Studios

United States

Arizona
VUE Gallery
336 Hwy. 179, Suite E101
Sedona, AZ 86336

California
CT Fine Furniture
San Diego, CA 92101
(by appointment)

del Mano Gallery
2001 Westwood Gallery
Los Angeles, CA 90025

Dovetail Collection
407 Healdsburg Ave.
Healdsburg, CA 95448

Espasso, Inc Gallery
8687 Melrose Ave. #B205
Los Angeles, CA 90069

Gallery M
328 Main St.
Half Moon Bay, CA 94019

Great Place
Between Ocean and 7th
Carmel, CA 93923

Siglo Moderno
8373 Melrose Avenue
Los Angeles, CA 90069

Stewart Kummer Gallery
35290 Old Stage Rd.
Gualala, CA 95445

William Zimmer Gallery
PO Box 263
Mendocino, CA 95460

Colorado
Anderson Art Ranch.
5263 Owl Creek Rd.
Snowmass Village, CO 81615

Connecticut
Black Creek Designs
26 Grove St.
New Canaan, CT 06840
(by appointment)

Silvermine Arts Guild
1037 Silvermine Rd.
New Canaan, CT 06840

Delaware
Creations Fine Woodworking Gallery
451 Hockessin Corner
Hockessin, DE 19707

Florida
BON, balance order nature
2100 Coral Way, Suite 100
Miami, FL 33145

Gallery Five
140 Bridge Road
Jupiter, FL 33469

Georgia
August Avery
Atlanta Decorative Arts Center
351 Peachtree Hills Ave. Suite 320
Atlanta, Georgia 30305

Naturalism Furniture
1564 DeKalb Ave. #5
Atlanta, GA 30307

Signature Shop & Gallery
3267 Roswell Road Northeast
Atlanta, GA 30305

Turner Custom Furniture
2383 Akers Mill Road SE #H9
Atlanta, GA 30339

Hawaii
Cliff Johns Gallery
76-5936 Mamalahoa Highway
Holualoa, HI 96725

Dennis Holzer Gallery
1169 Makawao Ave.
Makawao, HI 96768

Hana Coast Gallery
P.O. Box 565
Hana, HI 96713

Isaacs Art Center
65-1268 Kawaihae Rd.
Kamuela, HI

Na Pua Gallery
Grand Wailea Resort
3850 Wailea Alanui Dr.
Kihei, HI 96753

Volcano Art Center
PO Box 129
Volcano, HI 96785

Indiana
Swartzendruber Furniture Creations
17229 C.R. 18
Goshen, IN 46528

Kentucky
Kentucky Museum of Art and Craft
715 West Main St.
Louisville, KY 40202

Salvo Collective
216 S Shelby St.
Louisville, KY 40202

The Kentucky Artisan Center
200 Artisan Way
Berea, KY 40403

Maine
Messler Gallery at the Center for
Furniture Craftsmanship
25 Mill St.
Rockport, ME 04856

The Gallery at Frenchman's Bay
105 High St.
Ellsworth, ME 04605

Thos. Moser Showroom
149 Main St.
Freeport, ME 04032

Trinket and Fern
172 Middle St.
Portland, ME 04101

WallWork Gallery
67 Pascal Ave.
Rockport, ME 04856

Maryland
Garden Artisans
451 Defense Highway, Ste A
Annapolis, MD 21401

NeoCon East
Baltimore Convention Center One
West
Pratt St.
Baltimore, MD 21201

Massachusetts
Dane Gallery
28 Center St.
Nantucket, MA 02554

Gallery NAGA
67 Newbury St.
Boston, MA 02116

Half Crown Design & William Henry
Furniture
357 Huron Ave.
Cambridge MA 02138

Lexington Arts and Crafts Society
130 Waltham St.
Lexington, MA. 02421

MB Stahl Interiors
1381 Washington St.
West Newton, MA 02465

Mobilia Gallery
358 Huron Ave.
Cambridge, MA 02138

Shaw Cramer Gallery
56 Main St.
Vineyard Haven, MA 02568

Society of Arts and Crafts
175 Newbury St.
Boston, MA 02116

Michigan
The Artisans of Woodland Creek
4290 U.S. 31 North
Traverse City, MI 49686

Missouri
WoodShop Artisans
1303 E Cambridge
Springfield, MO 65804
(by appointment)

Nevada
Elan Collections
5235 W. Ponderosa Way #100
Las Vegas, NV 89118

New Hampshire
Doucette and Wolfe Furniture Makers
91 Hunting Ridge Rd.
Center Conway, NH 03813

New Hampshire Furniture Masters
PO 5733
Manchester, NH 03108

The Banks Gallery
420 Court St.
Portsmouth, NH 03801

New Mexico
Act One Gallery
218 Paseo Del Pueblo Norte # B
Taos, NM 87571

Jane Sauer Gallery
652 Canyon Rd.
Santa Fe, NM 87501

La Mesa of Santa Fe
225 Canyon Rd.
Santa Fe, NM 87501

Made in the Shade
418 Cerrillos Road # 1B
Santa Fe, NM 87501

Shidoni Gallery
P.O. Box 250
Tesuque NM 87574

New York
BeSpoke Global
New York, NY 10016

Design Lush
New York Design Center
200 Lexington Ave. Suite 415
New York, NY 10016

Downtown Design
184 Franklin St.
New York, NY 10013

Espasso, Inc.
38 N Moore
New York, NY 10013

Longhouse Reserve
133 Hands Creek Rd.
East Hampton, NY 11937

Mimosa Gallery
70 Beekman St. # C
Saratoga Springs, NY 12866

Pritam and Eames
29 Race Lane
East Hampton, NY 11937

Phillips De Pury, NOW exhibition: art
of 21st Century
450 West 15th St.
New York, NY 10011

Roskin Studio
Ancram, NY 12502
(by appointment)

Sharada Gallery
433 Warren St.
Hudson, NY 12534

SweetHeart Gallery
8 Tannery Brook Rd.
Woodstock, NY 12498

North Carolina
Grovewood Gallery
111 Grovewood Rd.
Asheville, NC 28804

Penland Gallery
3135 Conley Ridge Rd.
Penland, NC 28765

Piedmont Craftsmen
601 N Trade St # 100
Winston-Salem, NC 27101

Southern Highland Craft Guild
Milepost 382 Blue Ridge Parkway
Ashville, NC 28805

The Century Guild, Ltd.
PO Box 1117
Carrboro, NC 27510

Oregon
Inscapes Gallery
818 Southwest Bay Blvd.
Newport OR 97365

Real Mother Goose
901 SW Yamhill St.
Portland, OR 97205

Pennsylvania
Garden Accents
4 Union Hill Rd.
West Conshohocken, PA 19428

Handler Studio
3201 Fox St.
Philadelphia, PA 19129
(By appointment)

Moderne Gallery
111 North St.
Philadelphia, PA 19106

S.D. Feather
24 W. Walnut St.
Bethlehem, PA 18018

Society for Contemporary Craft
2100 Smallman St. # 1B
Pittsburgh, PA 15222

Index